W9-BMU-515

Toronto
Area by Area

Streetsmart

Within each Top 10 list in this book, no hierarchy
of quality or popularity is implied. All 10 are, in
the editor's opinion, of roughly equal merit.
    Throughout this book, floors are referred to in
accordance with American usage; i.e., the "first
floor" is at ground level.

Front cover and spine The Toronto skyline
featuring the CN Tower and the Rogers Centre
Back cover Niagara Falls viewed from the
Canadian side
Title page Our Game, a sculpture by Edie
Parker in front of the Hockey Hall of Fame on
Front Street, Toronto

**The information in this DK Eyewitness
Top 10 Travel Guide is checked regularly.**
Every effort has been made to ensure that
this book is as up-to-date as possible at the
time of going to press. Some details,
however, such as telephone numbers,
opening hours, prices, gallery hanging
arrangements, and travel information are
liable to change. The publishers cannot
accept responsibility for any consequences
arising from the use of this book, nor for any
material on third party websites, and cannot
guarantee that any website address in this
book will be a suitable source of travel
information. We value the views and
suggestions of our readers very highly. Please
write to: Publisher, DK Eyewitness Travel
Guides, Dorling Kindersley, 80 Strand, London
WC2R 0RL, Great Britain, or email
travelguides@dk.com

Welcome to
Toronto

Renowned museums and eclectic galleries; fine dining and cozy bistros; cobblestones and cutting-edge architecture; elegant department stores and quirky shops; a medieval-style castle with secret passageways; Niagara Falls within striking distance. Toronto is a city of contrasts, and with Eyewitness Top 10 Toronto it's yours to explore.

Toronto is a thriving metropolis that's home to one of the world's most multicultural populations. It has a contemporary vibe, yet the city is filled with historic treasures. The cobblestoned **Distillery Historic District** blends Victorian architecture with boutiques, galleries, and restaurants. The **St. Lawrence Market**, named the world's best market by *National Geographic* magazine, has been operating as a food emporium since 1803.

As for the city's modern-day persona, the safe, exciting downtown area has striking skyscrapers, fabulous shopping at the **CF Eaton Centre**, an array of family attractions such as the **Ripley's Aquarium of Canada**, and – honoring Canada's national pastime – the **Hockey Hall of Fame. Harbourfront**, stretching along Lake Ontario, provides hours of browsing pleasure. Catch the ferry here for the short sail to the scenic **Toronto Islands**.

Whether you're coming for a weekend or a week, our Top 10 guide brings together the best of everything that Toronto has to offer, from must-see attractions including the **CN Tower**, **Art Gallery of Ontario**, and **Casa Loma**, to chic shopping areas, hip clubs, and an array of restaurants that reflect the city's diversity. This guide has useful tips throughout, from seeking out what's free to avoiding the crowds, plus seven easy-to-follow itineraries designed to help you visit a clutch of sights in a short space of time. Add inspiring photography and detailed maps, and you've got the essential pocket-sized travel companion. **Enjoy the book, and enjoy Toronto.**

Clockwise from top: Toronto skyline, Art Gallery of Ontario, Ripley's Aquarium, Niagara Falls, the Stanley Cup in the Hockey Hall of Fame, National Bay Islands, Distillery Historic District

Exploring Toronto

Toronto offers a mosaic of attractions. These suggestions for a two- and four-day stay are designed so that visitors to the city can experience Toronto's most popular places in a short space of time. Many of the destinations are close to each other, so it's easy to mix and match. It's a good idea to pick a clear, sunny day for the CN Tower visit.

Ripley's Aquarium is home to a kaleidoscope of marine life.

Two Days in Toronto

Day ❶
MORNING
Head up the **CN Tower** *(see pp16–17)* for an incredible view of the city, the lake, and beyond. Then visit **Ripley's Aquarium** *(see pp28–9)* and check out some extraordinary marine life.
AFTERNOON
Walk to **Harbourfront** *(see pp66–9)* along Queens Quay. Take the ferry to the **Toronto Islands** *(see pp18–19)*, and enjoy the activities and the views.

Day ❷
MORNING
Start at **Union Station** *(see p43)* and walk up Bay Street, past the skyscrapers and the Romanesque-style **Old City Hall** *(see p78)*. Head to **CF Toronto Eaton Centre** *(see pp30–31)* to shop.
AFTERNOON
Take the Bay bus north to **Bloor Street** *(see p79)*, and have lunch in the Yorkville area. There are plenty of good choices on Cumberland Street and Yorkville Avenue. Walk

to the **Royal Ontario Museum** *(see pp12–13)* and enjoy the permanent collection and featured exhibition. Take a short cab ride or the subway (Museum station) north to **Casa Loma** *(see pp24–5)*, exiting at Dupont and then climb the stairs to the Gothic castle on the hill.

Four Days in Toronto

Day ❶
MORNING
Explore **Fort York** *(see p68)*, Canada's largest collection of War of 1812 buildings, then head to the **CN Tower**

Key
— Two-day itinerary
— Four-day itinerary

(see pp16–17) and **Ripley's Aquarium** *(see pp28–9)* to see what's under the sea.

AFTERNOON
Walk eastward along Front Street to **Union Station** *(see p43)*. Gaze up at the bank buildings. Continue north along Bay Street to **Old City Hall** *(see p78)*, before indulging in some retail therapy at the **CF Toronto Eaton Centre** *(see pp30–31)*.

Niagara Falls are a spectacular sight, especially when seen from a boat.

the picturesque **Niagara-on-the-Lake** *(see p101)*. If time allows, dine one of the town's fine restaurants and see a play at the Shaw Festival (summer).

Day ❷
MORNING
Explore the **Hockey Hall of Fame** *(see pp32–3)* then walk eastward to **St. Lawrence Market** *(see p90)*. Later, continue east to the **Distillery Historic District** *(see pp26–7)*, with its galleries, boutiques, and cafés.

AFTERNOON
From the Distillery, catch the 121 bus westbound, exiting at Blue Jay Way. Alongside the lake, at **Harbourfront** *(see pp66–9)*, stop off to visit the **Power Plant Contemporary Art Gallery** *(see p70)*. Catch the ferry to the **Toronto Islands** *(see pp18–19)* for a picnic.

Day ❸
MORNING
Visit **Niagara Falls** *(see pp34–7)* and, weather permitting, take a boat tour with Hornblower Cruises.

AFTERNOON
Visit the **Niagara Falls Butterfly Conservatory** *(see p35)*, then head to

Day ❹
MORNING
Visit the **Art Gallery of Ontario** *(see pp20–21)*, with its collections of Canadian and European art. Wander through **Chinatown** *(see p77)* and **Kensington Market** *(see p75)*. Both areas offer excellent lunch options.

AFTERNOON
Explore the **Royal Ontario Museum** *(see pp12–13)*. Afterwards, take a short cab ride or hop on the subway at Museum station and head north to **Casa Loma** *(see pp24–5)*, exiting at Dupont and climbing the stairs to the Gothic castle.

Casa Loma stands on a hill keeping a watchful eye over downtown.

Top 10 Toronto Highlights

The spectacular Horseshoe Falls roaring over the cliff at Niagara Falls

🔟 Toronto Highlights

As Canada's largest city and its financial hub, Toronto has a tremendous amount to offer, with a thriving arts scene, top museums, world-class restaurants and shops, and a beautiful lakeside location with lovely beaches. The city's cultural diversity, with over 90 ethnic groups, makes it a vibrant and exciting urban center.

Royal Ontario Museum ①

A treasure-trove of ancient mummies, exquisitely decorated period rooms, huge dinosaurs, stuffed birds, stunning Chinese art, and imposing Greek and Roman sculptures are among the many rewarding sights to be seen during a visit to this museum *(see pp12–15)*.

② CN Tower and its Views

High-speed external elevators mounted on this, the tallest building in the Western Hemisphere, whisk you up 181 stories to an unforgettable view of the city *(see pp16–17)*.

Toronto Islands ③

A short ferry ride from downtown, this chain of small islands provides a respite from summer heat with its beaches, picnic grounds, and amusement park *(see pp18–19)*.

④ Art Gallery of Ontario

This fabulous museum is home to an excellent collection of Canadian art, including that of contemporary artist Michael Snow. There are also fine collections of French Impressionists, Inuit art, sculpture, photography, and prints *(see pp20–21)*.

⑤ Casa Loma

Built by financier Sir Henry Pellatt, this turreted mansion, with grand rooms and beautiful gardens, offers a glimpse of turn-of-the-20th-century luxury *(see pp24–5)*.

DUPONT STREET

THE ANNEX

BLOOR STREET WE

SPADINA AVE

COLLEGE STREET

DUNDAS STREET WEST

AVENUE

QUEEN STREET WEST

KING STREET WES

SPADINA

FRONT STREET WES

GARDINER EXPRESSW
QUEENS QUAY WES

80 miles (130 km)

6 Distillery Historic District

Once the largest distillery in North America, this complex is one of Toronto's hottest destinations. Victorian buildings and cobblestoned streets provide a backdrop to the many unusual stores and galleries, and lovely restaurants and cafés found here (see pp26–7).

7 Ripley's Aquarium of Canada

Greet sharks, octopuses, stingrays, and giant grouper in this impressive aquarium. Start with the Canadian Waters gallery, home to an over-70-year-old lobster (see pp28–9).

8 CF Toronto Eaton Centre

Toronto's pre-eminent downtown mall, named after a now-defunct department-store chain, is located near major hotels and attractions. If you are looking for a one-stop shopping destination, this mall is it (see pp30–31).

9 Hockey Hall of Fame

Most visitors to Toronto who are ice-hockey fans make a pilgrimage here to see the original Stanley Cup, shoot pucks at a video goalie, walk through a re-created locker room, and watch some of hockey's sterling moments in the Broadcast Zone (see pp32–3).

10 Niagara Falls

After the 2-hour drive from Toronto, stand on Table Rock for a look at one of the world's wonders, the magnificent Horseshoe Falls, where the Niagara River plunges over a 188-ft (57-m) precipice. The town of Niagara Falls and the outlying area offer fine dining, entertainment, winery tours, museums, and more (see pp34–7).

YORKVILLE

0 meters   800
0 yards   800

CARLTON ST

DUNDAS ST EAST

DOWNTOWN

QUEEN STREET EAST

KING STREET EAST

HARBOURFRONT

Toronto Inner Harbour

Royal Ontario Museum

The Royal Ontario Museum, or ROM, was created in 1914 with the dual mandate of showcasing human civilization and the natural world. It is now Canada's largest museum, with over six million objects. Galleries of archeology, science, art, world cultures, and natural history display collections of Chinese treasures, mummy cases, and dinosaur skeletons. Hands-on exhibits invite kids to excavate for fossils and examine species under a microscope.

Futalognkosaurus Dinosaur ①
A dinosaur so big that he wouldn't fit inside the main exhibition hall, the Futalognkosaurus **(right)** greets visitors as they enter the museum lobby.

② Acropolis Model
This model of Greek temple life depicts the Parthenon and other buildings as they looked at the height of ancient Greek civilization.

③ Totem Poles
Four striking totem poles were carved out of western red cedar in the 1880s by the Haida and the Nisga'a peoples of Canada's northwest coast. The tallest is over 80 ft (24 m) high.

④ Djedmaatesankh Mummy
Decorated with hieroglyphics, this Egyptian sarcophagus **(left)**, dating back to c.850 BC, protects the mummified body of a court musician. The case has never been opened, but a CAT scan revealed this woman died aged 35 from a tooth abscess.

⑤ Chinese Guardian Lions
Two proud stone lions, which were carved for a Beijing palace in the 1600s, stand guard outside the museum.

NEED TO KNOW

MAP C3 ■ 100 Queen's Park (the main entrance is around the corner on Bloor St W) ■ 416 586 8000 ■ www.rom.on.ca

Open 10am–5:30pm daily (check website for Fri)

Adm $20 adults, $17 senior citizens, $15.50 students, $14 children aged 4–14; special exhibitions have a separate admission fee

■ The museum is very close to St. George and Museum subway stations

■ Grab a quick bite in the cafeteria on Basement Level 1.

■ Visit on Friday evenings for discounted admission. The website has special programing, much of which is free.

6 Living Beehive
This active beehive is a highlight of the Hands-On Biodiversity Gallery. See the interior of the hive, buzzing with honey bees that have flown in from outdoors.

Royal Ontario Museum

Key to Floorplan
Level 1
Level 2
Level 3

Mosaic Dome 7
A spectacular mosaic dome **(right)** tops the rotunda. Over a million tiny colored squares of Venetian glass form symbols of ancient cultures, such as an Inca thunder god and a mythical Greek seahorse.

8 English Parlor
Dating from the 1750s, with original carved pine walls and furniture, this parlor looks as if a wealthy gentleman and his card-playing friends have only momentarily left the room. Though the gilded harp in the corner is silent, some evocative, ambient Baroque music completes the vignette.

9 Hardwood Forest
The dappled light and hushed calm of an Ontario hardwood forest are perfectly re-created in this diorama. If you look closely, you will see more than 20 animals, among them a porcupine and fox.

10 Ming Tomb
Guarded by stone camels, a fierce warrior, and a scepter-bearing adviser, this ensemble of funerary sculpture **(below)** features artifacts from the Yuan dynasty (1271–1368), Ming dynasty (1368–1644), and Qing dynasty (1644–1912).

MUSEUM GUIDE

Walkways on each level join exhibitions in the Michael Lee-Chin Crystal to the main building. Level 1 includes the Korea, China, and Japan collections, and galleries exploring Canada's First Peoples and Canadian heritage. Natural history is the focus of Level 2, with galleries on gems and minerals, evolution, and dinosaurs. Level 3 features anthropology and archeology, with artifacts from Africa, the Americas, Asia Pacific, Egypt, and Rome, as well as 20th-century art and design. Textiles as well as the Institute for Contemporary Culture are on Level 4.

Royal Ontario Museum Collections

1 Dinosaurs

The Dinosaur Gallery, on Level 2 in the Michael Lee-Chin Crystal, is home to almost 25 full dinosaur skeletons, of both marine and land dwellers, including the world's most complete *Maiasaura* and her baby, which are thought to be 80 million years old.

2 Hands-On Biodiversity

Get up close with the wonders of the natural world in this imaginative discovery zone on Level 2. Touch animal skulls and pelts, and don special glasses to look at the world through the "eyes" of animals.

Paallirmiut clothing, Canada's First Peoples

Egyptian wall-cast sculpture

3 Ancient Egypt

More than 1,000 artifacts, from gold earrings to ceremonial mummy cases, combine to shed light on ancient Egypt (Level 3). A plaster cast taken from the temple of Queen Hatsheput near present-day Somalia, provides an opportunity to test your skill at decoding hieroglyphics.

4 Arms and Armor

On Level 3, battle gear stands guard over some 300 pieces – from 15th-century European chain mail to World War I automatic weapons – that highlight the history of human conflict.

5 Canada's First Peoples

The ROM's holdings of Indigenous artifacts, on Level 1, are superb. National treasures include an Innu-painted caribou-skin coat and a quilled pouch collected by Canadian painter Paul Kane (1810–71), who traveled among Native settlements in the mid-1800s. Don't miss the Umiak boat, which is large enough to hold an entire village.

6 Ice Age Mammals

The rise of mammals following the Ice Age's "big chill," which ended about 10,000 years ago, is explored in this dramatic exhibit on Level 2. A giant beaver, mastodon, saber-toothed cat, and hippopotamus are just some of the impressive specimens on display.

7 Gallery of Birds

Hundreds of birds from all over the world swoop together in one spectacular flock, suspended in mid-flight from the ceiling on Level 2. Marvel at the 9-ft (2.7-m) wing span of the albatross; listen to birdsongs at interactive booths; and pull out drawers containing nests, bones, eggs, and feathers.

8 Art Deco

Rare French and American Art Deco furniture, lamps, and sculpture (exquisitely crafted from ebony, lacquer, and ivory, among other fine materials) celebrate this influential design movement of the 1920s and 1930s. Art Deco glass, ceramic, and silver pieces round out this collection, on Level 3.

9 Greek Sculpture

Striking stone, bronze, and ivory sculptures make this collection on Level 3 one of the best in North

America. The pieces dating back to the Hellenistic Age, around 325 BC, reflect the development of Greek society under Alexander the Great, as his army forged into Egypt and India.

🔟 Chinese Art

Spanning over 6,000 years of Chinese history (4500 BC to AD 1900), this collection on Level 1 ranks among the world's finest. The procession of 7th-century ceramic tomb figures and the monumental Buddhist sculptures from the 12th to the 16th centuries are outstanding.

Ceramic figures, Chinese art gallery

THE CRYSTAL

The highlight of the museum's renovation is the Michael Lee-Chin Crystal, a magnificent addition designed by world-renowned architect Daniel Libeskind and named for the lead donor. This jagged crystalline structure of interlocking forms, with its spectacular atrium space, glass-sliver windows, and jutting angles thrusting over the sidewalk, now forms the dramatic entrance to the museum. Inside the Crystal, which has been designed to have no right angles, are four levels of galleries, including two unusual spaces: the Spirit House, a soaring void crisscrossed by bridges linking the newest galleries, and the Stair of Wonders, an intriguing vertical cabinet of curiosities from the ROM's collection. The Crystal is linked on all levels except the fourth to the original building.

The Royal Ontario Museum building is an engaging fusion of traditional and modern.

TOP 10 ARCHITECTURAL HIGHLIGHTS

1 Rotunda

2 Totem Poles

3 Queen's Park facade

4 Stained-glass windows, Queen's Park entrance

5 Spirit House

6 Liza's Garden

7 Floor mosaic at entrance to Samuel European Galleries

8 Leaded windows in the stairwells

9 Arched windows along western facade

10 Exterior cornice around building

🔟 ⭐ CN Tower and its Views

A 58-second elevator ride whisks you to the 114th story of the tallest building in the Western Hemisphere, the 181-story, 1,815-ft (553-m) communications tower built by Canadian National Railway in 1976. Breathtaking views from the glass-fronted elevator set the stage for more dizzying sights from the LookOut, where visitors can walk on the Glass Floor for a view 1,122 ft (342 m) straight down. For panoramic views 1,465 ft (447 m) above the ground, take an elevator up 33 more stories to the SkyPod, the highest observation level.

3 CF Toronto Eaton Centre
People flock here for the shops and eateries *(see pp30–31)*. The glass roof is modeled on a 19th-century Italian galleria.

4 Urban Forest
One look at Toronto from above and it's clear it's a green city: stately canopy trees line streets and snake along ravines.

1 City Hall
When opened in 1965, the building, with its two curving towers **(above)**, was controversial in conservative Toronto; it has since become a much-loved icon of the city's modern architecture *(see p77)*.

Fort York 2
Founded in 1793 and the site of the 1813 Battle of York, Fort York **(right)** has Canada's best collection of buildings from the War of 1812 era. Eight original structures still stand, but many buildings were torn down during the 1950s *(see p68)*.

5 Niagara Falls
If weather allows, you can see the mists rising above Niagara Falls, set 80 miles (130 km) to the southeast *(see pp34–7)*. The gentle curve of land along Lake Ontario reveals why the region is known as the Golden Horseshoe.

The distinctive CN Tower against the Toronto skyline

9 Toronto Music Garden

The garden's design, inspired by the music of Baroque composer J. S. Bach, is best seen from above; the swirling paths and plantings do indeed seem musical *(see p67)*.

10 Toronto Islands

This ribbon of islands **(below)** *(see pp18–19)* shelters Toronto's harbor and provides a car-free retreat just a short ferry ride from downtown. The islands have bike paths, picnic areas, beaches, and an amusement park *(see p48)*.

BUILDING FEATS

Considered one of the seven wonders of the modern world, the CN Tower is recognized as an unparalleled feat of modern engineering. It took 40 months to build the tower, with 1,537 workers working around the clock and pouring enough concrete to lay a sidewalk from Toronto to Kingston, 160 miles (260 km) away. A huge 10-ton Russian Sikorsky helicopter was used to lift the 44 pieces of the tower's 335-ft (102-m) antenna into place.

6 Roy Thomson Hall

The space-age design of this music hall **(above)**, located in the core of Toronto's theater district, features a distinctive glass canopy *(see p50)*.

7 Union Station

A relic from the days when passenger rail was the country's primary mode of transportation, this station has lost none of its grandeur since it opened in 1927, still serving as an impressive gateway to the city *(see p43)*.

8 Financial District

Soaring towers, such as those of the modernist Toronto-Dominion Centre *(see p68)*, signal the heart of Toronto's – and Canada's – financial district. The nation's major banks, insurance companies, and stockbrokers ply their trades, as wind-jostled workers hurry along the canyon-like streets.

NEED TO KNOW

MAP J5 ■ 301 Front St W ■ 416 868 6937 ■ www.cntower.ca

Open 9am–10:30pm daily; closed Dec 25

Adm $36 adults, $31 senior citizens and $26 children aged 4–12; add $12 for access to the SkyPod

■ Stop in at Horizons Restaurant on the LookOut level for casual fare, or reserve a table at the revolving 360 Restaurant (416 362 5411) to enjoy fine dining and a view that changes slowly throughout the meal.

■ Shop for one-of-a-kind souvenirs and authentic Canadiana at the Marketplace.

■ Test your nerve on the world's highest external walk on a building. CN Tower's EdgeWalk is a full-circle, hands-free walk on a 5-ft- (1.5-m-) wide ledge.

TOP 10 ★ Toronto Islands

The islands were formed when the rushing waters of the Don River separated a spit from the mainland during a storm in 1858. There are over a dozen islets and mid-sized islands in this archipelago, some of them connected by bridges, others accessible only by boat. A thriving community of creative characters calls Algonquin and Ward's islands home, while Centre Island is very popular for its amusement park. No cars are allowed here, adding to the tranquil charm. Along with walking, two great ways to get around are to hire a bike or rent a boat and paddle through the lagoon system.

CANADA'S CONEY ISLAND

Hanlan Point's heyday began in the 1880s as city dwellers flocked to its vaudeville theater, amusement park, dance hall, and hotels. Twenty years later, thousands of fans cheered on the baseball legend Babe Ruth as he hit his first professional home run, on September 5, 1914, at Hanlan Point's new stadium. By the end of 1937, however, the stadium and the fading resort had been torn down to make way for the Island Airport.

1 Ward's Island
Over 700 people live here in what began, in the 1880s, as a tiny tent settlement **(above)**. Stroll along the pathways and marvel at the creative ways in which the cottages have been adorned to the owners' tastes.

2 Ferry
Enjoy one of the best views to be had of the Toronto skyline aboard a ferry **(below)**, dating back to the 1950s, as it chugs across the lake to the Toronto Islands.

3 The Rectory
This restaurant also functions as Ward's Island social center. Main courses, soups, salads, and sandwiches are healthy and hearty, and the desserts are delicious.

7 Algonquin Island

The creativity of the islands' residents is most exuberantly expressed in their quirky, colorful gardens, which are in delightful bloom in the warmer months. The green thumb enthusiasts of Algonquin Island are often happy to share their tips with passersby.

10 Gibraltar Point Lighthouse

The oldest lighthouse in the city **(below)** has served as a shipping beacon since the early 19th century. The historic lime-stone landmark is rumored to be haunted by the ghost of its first keeper.

4 Far Enough Farm

Kids will love feeding and petting the lambs, goats, cows, pigs, and other farm animals **(above)** at this small petting zoo.

8 Boardwalk

The 1.5-mile (2.5-km) boardwalk runs from Ward's Island to Centre Island and is great for a lakeside stroll.

Toronto Islands

5 Bicycling

The best way to tour the islands is on wheels along the pedestrian-bicycle trails stretching the 4-mile (6-km) archipelago. Rent a one-person or tandem bike or quadracycle **(below)**.

6 Centreville Amusement Park

This small amusement park on Centre Island has more than 30 rides, including swan boats and a colorful 1890s carousel (see p48).

9 Hanlan's Point

The point's two sandy beaches are pop-ular with sunbathers. In 1999, one of the beaches reclaimed the clothing-optional status that it enjoyed when it first opened in 1894 (see p53).

NEED TO KNOW

MAP B6–E6

Ferry: 416 397 2628; www.torontoislands.org

Bicycling: 416 203 0009; www.torontoisland bicyclerental.com

■ There are fast-food spots and snack bars on the islands, but keep in mind that these are well spread out and have seasonal hours.

■ Ferries depart from the terminal at the foot of Bay St. Centre Island ferries operate summer and fall; Ward's Island and Hanlan's Point ferries run year-round.

■ The ferry ride ($7.71 adults, $3.72 children aged 2–14; return) takes about 10 minutes. Bikes are permitted on board, except on the Centre Island boat if it's busy.

🔟 ⭐ Art Gallery of Ontario

Founded in 1900, the wide-ranging Art Gallery of Ontario (AGO) has over 80,000 works. The outstanding pieces of Canadian art, in particular paintings by the Group of Seven, are a national treasure. Along with superb Henry Moore plasters, bronzes, and other works, the gallery exhibits significant masterpieces of European art, from paintings by Tintoretto and Frans Hals to Vincent van Gogh and Pablo Picasso. More recent acquisitions include an impressive collection of African and Australian Aboriginal art.

Group of Seven ①

Canadian landscapes epitomize these artists who strove, in the 1920s, to create a national artistic identity. The gallery's collection features works by MacDonald **(right)**, Jackson, Johnston, and Harris, among others.

② Canadian Collection

These galleries include First Nations and Inuit art, and such Canadian luminaries as Emily Carr **(above)**, William Kurelek, and Alex Colville.

④ Photography

This collection has early work, with a large contribution from Czech photographer Josef Sudek, and photographs taken in the 1930s and 40s by the Klinsky Press Agency.

⑤ Inuit Art

This fine collection of works produced after World War II includes sculptures **(below)** and wall hangings made from indigenous materials.

③ Thomson Collection

This philanthropic cultural gift with 2,000 works adds remarkable depth to the AGO's collection, with emphasis on Tom Thomson and the Group of Seven, as well as 19th-century painters Cornelius Krieghoff and Paul Kane.

6 Contemporary

Accessed by the wooden spiral staircase, this collection covers American and European art since

1900 and Canadian art since 1985. Canadian artists represented here include Joanne Tod, Betty Goodwin, and Elizabeth Magor. Conceptual artists include Michael Snow **(left)** and Jeff Wall.

7 The AGO Kids' Gallery

This child-friendly gallery has themed exhibitions geared at young visitors. There's also an activity center, costumes, and a photo booth where kids can draw and pose for portraits of themselves.

8 Henry Moore

The world's largest public collection of works by British artist Henry Moore (1898–1986) encompasses bronze sculptures, plaster and bronze maquettes, drawings, and prints. His monumental *Large Two Forms* takes its place outdoors, with its surface now worn smooth by admirers' countless rubbings.

THE GRANGE

Set at the south end of the art gallery, the Grange was the first home of the AGO and was given National Historic Site status in 1970. The elegant Georgian mansion was constructed in 1817, when Toronto was just the small town of York in Upper Canada, and it reflects the conservative British tastes of the region at the time with its symmetrical five-bay facade and central pediment.

9 French Impressionists

Claude Monet, Camille Pissarro, and Pierre-Auguste Renoir **(above)** are just some of the 19th-century artists whose masterpieces grace this estimable collection.

10 Prints and Drawings

The works in this collection range from the 15th to the 21st centuries and include important Italian, Dutch, German, French, and British pieces. *Adam and Eve* (1504) by German artist Albrecht Dürer is a highlight. Works by Canadians also feature strongly.

NEED TO KNOW

MAP J3 ■ 317 Dundas St W ■ 416 979 6648 ■ www.ago.net

Open 10:30am–5:30pm Tue, Thu, Sat, & Sun (to 9pm Wed & Fri)

Adm $19.50 adults, $11 youths and students, $16 senior citizens, $49 family ticket, under 5s free

■ The AGO features a lower level café with a family-friendly light lunch menu and the upmarket Frank, where artful dining is embraced by pairing menus with exhibitions.

■ Browse the Gallery Shop for specialty gifts, reproductions from the gallery's collection, books, and handcrafted jewelry.

■ Join one of the free tours for extra insight into the collections and exhibits. Call the information line for details.

TOP 10 ★ Casa Loma

This Edwardian-style castle, completed in 1914 for a staggering $3.5 million, looms on a hill, overlooking downtown. Designed by famed Toronto architect E. J. Lennox (responsible for many of Toronto's historic buildings), Casa Loma – Spanish for "house on the hill" – was the estate of prominent financier and industrialist Sir Henry Pellatt, who was forced by financial ruin to abandon his 98-room dream home less than 10 years after it was built.

1 Towers

Stunning views reward those not afraid of heights. Climb up to the top and survey the property from its highest perch. The east tower **(below)** is based on Scottish castle design, while the west tower, of Norman design, offers a breathtaking view of the city.

2 Sir Henry's Bathroom

This room is heavy on hedonistic comfort, with the shower designed to completely surround the body with sprays of water from above and from the sides, and six large taps controlling three levels of pipes. The walls are made of Carrara marble.

3 Sir Henry's Study

The wood panels by the fireplace conceal two secret passages. The one to the right gave Sir Henry quick access to the wine cellar and his huge wine collection. The one to the left emerged on the second floor, near his bedroom suite.

4 Great Hall

The grand entrance hall **(below)**, with its 60-ft- (18-m-) high ceiling, sets the castle's tone of splendor. Gargoyles grin down on visitors from the pillars. Audio guide tapes are available here.

Previous pages The magnificent Casa Loma

7 Conservatory
Magnificent bronze-and-glass doors, each set costing $10,000, are reproductions of a set made for an Italian villa. The intricate stained-glass ceiling dome, from Italy, was originally backlit by 600 light bulbs, so that it glowed at night **(left)**.

FIRST IN LUXURY

As the founder of the Toronto Electric Light Company, Sir Henry Pellatt brought electric power to the city, so it is not surprising that his home featured a range of innovations that enhanced comfort on a scale never before seen in a Canadian home. These included an electric lighting system controlled from a panel in Sir Henry's bedroom, a central vacuuming system, forced-air heating, and the city's first electric elevator in a private home.

9 Round Room
With doors and windows custom-bowed to align with the curved walls, this lovely room is furnished with period pieces. Sir Pellatt's suite of carved Louis XV chairs and folding screen are upholstered in rare French tapestry.

5 Oak Room
It took artisans 3 full years to carve the magnificent French oak paneling in this drawing room **(above)**. The plaster ceiling moldings conceal indirect lighting – the first time this type of lighting was used in a Canadian home.

6 Tunnel
Beneath the floors, a tunnel connects the castle to the carriage house and stables, where horses were kept in style. An exhibit tells the story of the city's dark days, including the Plague, the Prohibition, and the Depression.

8 Library
Stripes of light and dark wood in the herringbone oak floor create an optical illusion of different shadings from each end of the room. The elaborate plaster ceiling features portrait busts and the family's coats of arms.

10 Gardens
Lavish gardens **(above)**, punctuated by sculptures and fountains, grace the estate with blooms in season. Eight themed areas range from formal rose beds to woodland with luscious spring wild flowers.

🔟 ⭐ Distillery Historic District

Walking the pedestrian-only cobblestone streets past the beautifully preserved Victorian industrial architecture, you'll feel as if you've stumbled into another century. The buildings of this 13-acre (5-ha) site were, until 1990, part of Gooderham and Worts, once the world's largest distillery; the distillery evolved from a grist mill founded here in 1832. The 150-year-old district has been infused with new life and is a vibrant area of cafés, restaurants, galleries, art studios, performance venues, and specialty shops.

1 Boiler House Complex
In the 1860s, the boiler house heated the entire distillery. Other buildings in the complex housed a carpentry shop, a blacksmith, and a canteen. They have now been converted into restaurants and a bakery.

2 Corkin Gallery
Fronted with huge windows to let in natural light and diminish the fire hazard of producing alcohol under gas lighting, this 1873 building (above) is the perfect setting for the art and photography exhibitions within.

NEED TO KNOW

MAP E5 ■ 55 Mill St ■ Take the 504 King streetcar or Parliament St bus 65 from Castle Frank to King and Parliament, then walk south on Parliament ■ www.the distillerydistrict.com

■ Many of the district's restaurants and cafés have large patios set amongst the historic buildings. With no traffic or exhaust fumes, the Distillery District is a perfect place to dine on a summer evening.

■ Join a guided tour ($19) or a Segway tour ($39 for 30 minutes; $69 for an hour) to get the most out of your visit. Details at www.segwayofontario. com or call 416 642 0008.

■ The district hosts many festivals and events throughout the summer and a popular Christmas Market in December.

3 Balzac's Coffee
The pumps in this building were connected to the underground reservoir, in case of fire; others were used for alcohol. It is now home to Balzac's Coffee; beans are roasted Mondays and Fridays (above).

4 Bergo Designs
Though expensive, this design shop has some of the district's most interesting items and is worth a browse.

6 Young Centre for the Performing Arts

Housed in Tank House No. 9 and No. 10 **(left)**, where whiskey was stored while it aged, this is the main performance space of Soulpepper, the city's largest theater company *(see p51).*

9 Artscape Distillery Studios

The majority of arts organizations and artists in the distillery complex have their offices, workshops, and studios in these brick-fronted buildings where liquor was once stored.

Distillery Historic District

7 Arta Gallery

Located just off Parliament Street, and with the same old-world charm as the district itself, this gallery occupies a building that once housed a huge tank of molasses for rum.

8 Mill Street Brewery

While many of the distillery buildings still smell faintly of the grain and alcohol once stored within, this 1879 building renews its scent of malt and hops daily, from the Mill Street Brewery. Traditional handcrafted beers include an organic lager and a robust coffee porter. While sipping samples, check out the display of vintage distilling equipment.

5 Caffe Furbo

This quaint café **(below)** in the heart of the district occupies a building once used for canning industrial-grade alcohol. It now offers both delicious food and art to enjoy with it.

10 Thompson Landry Gallery

This gallery, showcasing Quebec artists, is set in a huge limestone structure, the oldest in the complex. Its exterior still retains features, such as a winch, from the days when the lakeshore – and ships – came right up to the building.

FILMING AT THE DISTILLERY

When the Gooderham and Worts Distillery ceased operations in 1990, the entire site, with its wonderfully evocative atmosphere, began a new life as the largest film set outside Hollywood. Hundreds of film shoots took place here during the 1990s, including *Chicago*, *The Hurricane*, and *X-Men*, along with popular television series such as *La Femme Nikita* and *Alfred Hitchcock Presents*, making this Canada's busiest filming location.

TOP 10 ⭐ Ripley's Aquarium of Canada

Crouched at the base of the CN Tower, this hulking wave-like structure opened in 2013. Inside, over 16,000 marine animals glide and float within stunningly displayed fresh- and saltwater tanks, some several stories deep, others floating overhead. The Discovery Centre has play equipment for when the kids start to feel fished-out. Whether you're surrounded on all sides by saw-tooth fish or getting to know a zebra shark from a perspex bubble, it's great fun.

1 Sea Dragons, The Gallery

At first glance, you may only notice elaborate seaweed. Look again. Otherworldly weedy and leafy sea dragons float gracefully by **(above)**.

2 Piranhas

These deceptively peaceful, glittering predators have their own tank.

3 Rainbow Reef

A wonderful sea of color awaits at this Indo-Pacific reef **(above)** where vibrant coral competes with an array of neon species of fish.

4 Discovery Centre

Pet a horseshoe crab at the touch pool and surround yourself with clown fish in the peek-a-boo tanks **(above)**. A water table with locks, dams, and fish-runs demonstrates the complexity of shipping going through the Great Lakes.

NEED TO KNOW

MAP J5 ■ 288 Bremner Blvd ■ 647 351 3474 ■ www.ripleyaquariums.com/canada

Open 9am–11pm daily (on some days it closes earlier for private functions; check the website)

Adm $29.98 adults, $19.98 senior citizens and youths (6–13), $9.98 children aged 3–5

■ Light bites such as hot dogs, pizza, and coffee are available at Ripley's® Café inside the aquarium.

■ During the school year, weekdays can be busier than you might expect. Avoid most school groups by arriving after 2pm.

Ripley's Aquarium of Canada

Key to Floorplan
Lower Level
Upper Level

AQUARIUM GUIDE

Start on the Upper Level with Canadian Waters. A ramp winds around the Pacific Kelp down to the Dangerous Lagoon and then on to the Discovery Centre. Continue on to Perfect Predators and through Planet Jellies to the ramp back up to the Upper Level past the filtration systems of the Life Support System. Exit via the gift shop.

9 Planet Jellies
The stars of the gallery, the Pacific Sea Nettle jellyfish **(above)** put on a stunning display of contrasting colors.

5 Great Lakes, Canadian Waters
Bass, pike, carp, trout, catfish, and the comical longnose gar – visitors may be surprised to see just how large the fish from the Great Lakes Basin can grow.

6 Ray Bay
Graceful Southern, Cownose, and Roughtail rays seem to fly through the waters. The floor-to-ceiling tank gives the rays plenty of room to swoop and dive, skimming right past the faces of dazzled observers.

7 Swarm: Nature by Numbers
A thrilling showcase of 1,000 new animals that swarm, including schools of coral catfish and mobs of blue blubber jellyfish.

10 Pacific Kelp, Canadian Waters
Strands of kelp provide a roomy home for over 25 species that swim off Canada's West Coast.

8 Dangerous Lagoon
A 315-ft (96-m) underwater tunnel takes visitors through the aquarium's largest tank **(below)** where sharks steal the show.

TOP10 ⭐ CF Toronto Eaton Centre

This upscale mall is named for Canadian retail legend Timothy Eaton, whose department store, Eaton's, was a national institution until 1999, when the company declared bankruptcy. Big, busy, and boisterous, this quintessential downtown mall was opened in 1977 and heralded as the anchor that would transform down-at-heel Yonge and Dundas streets into an upscale destination. The complex now houses some 230 stores, restaurants, and cafés, including Canada's first Saks Fifth Avenue and Toronto's first Nordstrom.

1 Flight Stop
Suspended in the central atrium is this sculpted gaggle of geese by Toronto artist Michael Snow, so life-like that you almost expect to hear the birds honk.

2 The Labyrinth
This circuitous grass path is modeled on the 13th-century labyrinth at Chartres Cathedral in France.

3 Fountain
A focal point of the mall, this waterburst fountain **(below)** lulls visitors with soothing sounds of falling water, then astonishes as water shoots 100 ft (30 m) into the air. Surrounded by benches, the fountain is a good spot for a break.

5 Galleria
Natural light pours through the soaring glass roof into the arcade **(above)**, designed by Eb Zeidler and modeled on the 19th-century Galleria Vittorio Emanuele in Milan. Nordstrom is located at the north end, while Hudson's Bay and Saks Fifth Avenue anchor the south end.

4 Scadding House
Built in 1857 for the Church of the Holy Trinity's first rector, this Georgian-Gothic house was moved here to make way for the mall. The church and house may be Yonge Street's oldest building complex. The current rector lives in the house.

DUNDAS ST WEST DUNDAS ST EAST

DUNDAS SQUARE

YONGE ST

QUEEN ST WEST

CF Toronto Eaton Centre

7 Church of the Holy Trinity

This Anglican church **(left)** dating to 1847 is an oasis of calm amid the commercial bustle. Admire the turreted entranceway and then step inside to see the stained-glass windows.

8 Hudson's Bay

Canada's largest department store chain, Hudson's Bay sells a wide selection of merchandise but might be best known for its point blankets, first used to barter for beaver pelts with the Cree of the First Nations. Its trading posts, based in the vast north of what is now Canada, were influential centers of commerce.

9 Bronze Plaque

This historic plaque commemorates Yonge Street, ranked the longest street in the world by the Guinness Book of World Records. Yonge Street divides East and West Toronto and is the site of the city's first subway line.

6 PATH

From the CF Toronto Eaton Centre you can access the 18-mile (30-km) or so underground walkway PATH. Linking several main attractions, PATH winds through stores and food courts.

10 Yonge-Dundas Square

Toronto's once-tawdry intersection is now a public square **(below)** embellished with 22 fountains. Events take place here, especially during the summer.

HUDSON'S BAY COMPANY (HBC)

The HBC controlled the continent's lucrative fur trade for 200 years. It was so powerful that it made laws and even waged war with Native tribes. After years of fierce English-French battles over its posts, it lost its monopoly, and, in 1870, it sold its land to the Government of Canada. Moving to retail, the HBC opened its first store in 1881, but kept a hand in the fur trade until 1991, when its last fur salon closed.

NEED TO KNOW

MAP L3 ▪ 220 Yonge St (alternative entrances along Yonge St between Dundas and Queen, and at Queen St west of Yonge St) ▪ 416 598 8560 ▪ www.toronto eatoncentre.com

Open 10am–9:30pm Mon–Fri, 9:30am–9:30pm Sat, 10am–7pm Sun; closed Dec 25

▪ The Urban Eatery in the basement at the north end of the mall has a range of food counters. Trinity Square Café, in the Church of the Holy Trinity, is open weekdays for lunch.

▪ Take a ride up the Eaton Center's glass elevators, located near the central fountain, for a wonderful view of the galleria from above.

▪ Navigate PATH using the color-coded signs: the red P steers you south, the orange A west, the blue T north, and the yellow H east.

🔟 ⭐ Hockey Hall of Fame

This shrine to Canada's favorite sport is housed in part of a beautiful former bank building dating to 1885, and it contains the most comprehensive collection of hockey memorabilia in the world, among which is the original Stanley Cup trophy. Interactive exhibits run the gamut from multimedia trivia kiosks that test your hockey knowledge to a virtual-reality puck-shooting game that allows visitors to go one-on-one against life-size, animated versions of top players.

① Stanley Cup

One of the world's best-known trophies, the original Stanley Cup is on display here, as is the current one. Named for the country's sixth Governor General, it was first presented in 1893.

② Montreal Canadiens Locker Room

The only thing missing from this re-created locker room **(below)** from the old Montreal Forum is the players.

③ Goalie Mask Exhibit

This fun display includes several strange examples of face protection **(left)** that have been personalized by goalies over the years.

④ Game Time Zone

On a faux ice rink, with arena boards and multimedia scoreboard, shoot a puck at a life-sized video-projection goalie, or be the goalie facing simulated shots by greats Sidney Crosby and Alexander Ovechkin.

⑤ Great Hall

Players and icons of hockey are celebrated in this 45-ft- (14-m-) high former banking hall **(above)**. Giants of the game appear on the Honoured Members Wall, and all major NHL trophies are on display.

NEED TO KNOW

MAP L5 ■ 30 Yonge St (enter through Brookfield Place concourse) ■ 416 360 7765 ■ www.hhof.com

Open daily (hours vary seasonally); closed Jan 1, Dec 25 and induction day.

Adm $18 adults, $14 senior citizens, $12 children, under 4s free

■ Many of the eateries in Brookfield Place *(see p42)* have seating in the spectacular galleria. A food court on the lower

level provides snacks for on the go.

■ If your energy flags, take a seat in one of the Hall of Fame's two theater venues to watch a retrospective highlights video or a multimedia presentation.

Hockey Hall of Fame

Key to Floorplan
- Main level
- Upper level

CANADA'S GAME

Though many countries claim to have invented ice hockey, Canada calls the game its own. Even so, its origins are hotly contested. Some credit King's College students in Windsor, Nova Scotia, with putting puck to ice in the 1800s; others credit Micmac Indians around the same period. Whatever the origin, British soldiers at the garrison in Halifax, Nova Scotia, were playing the game by the 1850s.

8 Movie Theaters

The Hall of Fame's two theaters screen full-length games and highlights. You can also enjoy hockey's first 3-D movie, Stanley's Game Seven.

6 Broadcast Zone

Thanks to state-of-the-art technology, visitors can experience the TV broadcast world from different angles, both on and off the camera, including calling the play-by-play or testing sports anchor skills in front of a camera.

7 Our Game

Exuberant young players leap over the boards for a hockey game in this larger-than-life bronze sculpture (below) by Ontario artist Edie Parker. Located just outside the museum at Yonge and Front streets, it is a popular backdrop for photographs.

9 Golden Goal Display

The Golden Goal exhibit features Sidney Crosby's podium, "Golden Net," stick, puck, and gloves from the 2010 Winter Olympics (above).

10 Spirit of Hockey Shop

The museum's exit takes visitors through this shop. Hockey-themed merchandise includes a wide selection of team jerseys, sticks, and other items printed with logos.

TOP 10 ⭐ Niagara Falls

One of the world's most famous natural attractions, Niagara Falls is a dazzling spectacle of great arcs of hissing, frothing water crashing over cliffs 20 stories high. Drifting spray adds to the excitement of being near the edge of a stomach-churning drop. The 188-ft- (57-m-) high Canadian Horseshoe Falls is the mightiest of the three cataracts that make up the falls, while across the Niagara River lie the American Falls and the smaller Bridal Veil Falls. When visiting, take time to stop at some of the other sights in the region, including its renowned vineyards, historic museums, and the small, charming town of Niagara-on-the-Lake.

1 Voyage to the Falls
Experience the mighty falls from below on a Hornblower Niagara Cruise. The 20-minute voyage takes you to the Great Gorge, American Falls, Bridal Veil Falls, and into the spray of Horsehoe Falls.

2 American Falls
New York State, on the US side of the inter-national border, lays claim to this cataract. Its 950-ft- (290-m-) wide crest sees only a fraction of the volume of water that is carried over by the Horseshoe Falls.

3 Journey Behind the Falls
Rock tunnels behind the Horseshoe Falls lead you past a wall of water so thick it blocks out day-light. The vantage point, below the gorge's rim, is inspiring **(below)**. Rain ponchos are provided.

Niagara Falls

4 The Old Scow
Shipwrecked in 1918, this barge is now stranded on rocks. The two-man crew survived but had to wait 29 hours near the brink of the falls before being rescued.

8 Whirlpool Rapids

A sharp turn in the river just downstream of the falls creates a raging whirlpool. Look down on the rapids from a cable-car **(left)** traversing this lethal stretch of water.

5 Horseshoe Falls

This 2,200-ft- (670-m-) wide cataract is formed as 90 percent of the water of the Niagara River, the outlet from Lake Erie to Lake Ontario, roars over a semicircular cliff of the Niagara Escarpment **(below)**.

FORCEFUL FLOW

The forces of erosion that created the falls are today responsible for wearing them away. Before hydroelectric stations were built on the Niagara River, the rock face eroded by up to 6 ft (1.8 m) a year. It is now just 1 ft (30 cm) annually. Almost a fifth of the Earth's freshwater flows over the falls – so much that it is thought that it would take only an hour to fill a ditch between Canada's east and west coasts.

6 Butterfly Conservatory

The conservatory is a huge heated dome with thousands of colorful creatures **(below)** flitting freely about – and sometimes landing on delighted visitors.

9 Table Rock

Stand mere feet from Horseshoe Falls, only a rail between you and a torrent of water. The lookout point was so named because it extended over the gorge like a table leaf. Deemed unstable in 1935, the ledge was blasted off.

10 Niagara Parks Botanical Gardens

These beautiful gardens, 6 miles (9 km) from the falls, include a splendid rose display with more than 2,000 varieties.

7 White Water Walk

Descend from the top of the chasm by elevator to a tunnel leading to a riverside boardwalk. The whirlpools and rapids here are among the most spectacular, and treacherous, in the world.

NEED TO KNOW
MAP Q3

Tourist Info: 5400 Robinson St; 905 356 6061 or 1 800 563 2557; discount passes available online; www.niagarafallstourism.com

Voyage to the Falls: $25.95 adults, $15.95 children; age 4 and under free; www.niagaracruises.com

■ Windows by Jamie Kennedy (www.windowsbyjamiekennedy.com) offers fine dining with great views of the falls.

■ The Adventure Pass includes a Hornblower Cruise, Journey Behind the Falls, White Water Walk, Niagara's Fury, and WEGO shuttle bus rides (www.niagaraparks.com).

Fun Things to Do Around Niagara

1 Fallsview Casino Resort

6380 Fallsview Blvd, Niagara Falls ▪ 1 888 325 5788 ▪ Open 24 hrs daily

Try your luck at the largest gaming resort in Canada, with 3,000 slot machines, 130 gaming tables, hotel, spa, shops, and restaurants.

All the fun of the fair at Clifton Hill

2 Clifton Hill

Niagara Falls

This is the center of Niagara Falls' entertainment, home to museums, mini-golf, and Midway, with hotels and restaurants for all budgets.

3 Helicopter Tours

Niagara Helicopters (10 mins), 1 800 281 8034; National Helicopters (20 mins), 1 800 491 3117

Experience the exhilaration of swooping over the falls.

4 IMAX Theatre Niagara Falls

6170 Fallsview Blvd, Niagara Falls ▪ 866 405 4629 ▪ www.imaxniagara.com

Niagara: Miracles, Myths and Magic chronicles the history of the falls. Projected onto a giant screen, the movie makes you feel like you're right in the midst of things. Original stunt barrels are displayed in the theater's Daredevil Gallery.

5 Welland Canal

Lock 3 Viewing Complex & Museum: Government Rd, St. Catharines ▪ 1 800 305 5134 ▪ Open 9am–5pm daily

Linking Lake Ontario and Lake Erie, this eight-lock, 27-mile (43-km) canal opened in 1829, allowing vessels to traverse the Niagara Escarpment – and the 328-ft (100-m) difference in height between the lakes. The canalside trail from Thorold to St. Catharines is great for ship-gazing.

6 Queenston Heights Park

Niagara River Pkwy, Niagara Falls

A monument pays tribute to General Brock, a leader of the British forces killed in battle here during the War of 1812, when the US invaded Upper Canada *(see p68)*. With great views of Niagara River, the park is an excellent spot for a picnic.

7 Old Fort Erie

350 Lakeshore Rd, Ft Erie ▪ 905 871 0540 ▪ Open mid-May–Oct: 10am–5pm daily ▪ Adm

This reconstructed fort, which was a supply base for British troops in the 1700s, was also the site of many battles with US forces throughout the 1800s.

8 Skylon Tower

5200 Robinson St ▪ 905 356 2651 ▪ Open 8am–midnight daily (summer); 9am–midnight (winter) ▪ Adm

A viewing deck affording vistas of as far as 80 miles (130 km), this tower rises 775 ft (236 m) above the falls. The popular revolving restaurant offers fine dining.

Revolving dining, Skylon Tower

Re-enactment at Fort George

9 Fort George

51 Queen's Parade, Niagara-on-the-Lake ▪ 905 468 6614 ▪ Open May–Aug: 10am–5pm daily; Sep–Apr: noon–4pm Sat & Sun ▪ Adm

This historic British fort, built in 1796, was a key defense post during the War of 1812 between Britain and the US *(see p68)*. It has been restored to the period, with replica buildings and costumed staff playing host.

10 MarineLand

7657 Portage Rd, Niagara Falls ▪ 905 356 9565 ▪ Admission booths open 10am–5pm late May–mid-Oct, park open until nightfall ▪ Adm

Visitors can hop on the ten-plus rides at this family-friendly theme park, including a looping roller coaster and Sky Screamer, a triple tower ride with views of the Falls.

DAREDEVIL FEATS

For some 200 years, daredevils have risked their lives at Niagara Falls. Many have had close calls; 19 have died. The first daredevil, Sam Patch, dove headfirst from an 85-ft-(26-m-) high platform into the churning Niagara River in 1829 and survived. Ten days later he did it again, from a height of 130 ft (40 m). The Great Blondin crossed the gorge on a tightrope nine times in 1859. When Blondin returned in 1860 for more stunts, such as pushing a wheelbarrow across the rope, he was challenged by a young upstart, the Great Farini, who crossed carrying a washing machine. Farini became increasingly daring, doing headstands and hanging by his toes. He survived them all and died at the age of 91. The first woman funambulist, Maria Spelterini, crossed blindfolded, in 1876. The first woman to survive going over the falls in a barrel was Annie Taylor, in 1901.

TOP 10 NIAGARA DAREDEVILS

1 Jean Francois Gravelot, aka The Great Blondin, tightrope crossing, 1859

2 Guillermo Antonio Farini, aka The Great Farini, stilt tightrope crossing, 1864

3 Henry Bellini, tightrope crossing and leap into river, 1873

4 Maria Spelterini, first woman to cross on a tightrope, 1876

5 Carlisle Graham, first man over the falls in a barrel, 1886

6 Clifford Calverly, fastest tightrope crossing, 1887

7 James Hardy, youngest tightrope crosser (21), 1896

8 Annie Edson Taylor, first woman over the falls in a barrel, 1901

9 Lincoln Beachy, first airplane stunt at the falls, 1911

10 Nik Wallenda, tightrope crossing, 2012

Blondin couldn't get enough of Niagara Falls, crossing on a tightrope many times.

The Top 10
of Everything

The Michael Lee-Chin Crystal extension
at the Royal Ontario Museum

Museums and Galleries

1 Royal Ontario Museum

Canada's foremost museum offers an excellent balance of art, archeology, science, and nature, with over six million artifacts in its collections *(see pp12–15)*.

2 Gardiner Museum of Ceramic Art

Founded in 1984 by Canadian collectors George and Helen Gardiner, the museum showcases their collection of pre-Columbian American pottery and European porcelain. Later additions include Asian ceramics and contemporary art *(see p78)*.

Figure, Gardiner Museum of Ceramic Art

3 McMichael Canadian Art Collection

The outstanding Group of Seven collection features at this gallery. The Group endeavored, in the early 20th century, to express a national identity through their paintings of the Canadian wilderness *(see p96)*.

4 Power Plant Contemporary Art Gallery

Known for its boundary-pushing contemporary Canadian and international art, this edgy, non-collecting gallery features rotating shows of consistently high quality. If the art sometimes mystifies visitors, at least the building is instantly recognizable: a brick smokestack tops the 1920s converted power station *(see p70)*.

5 Art Gallery of Ontario

Reflecting some 600 years of human creative endeavor, the gallery's permanent collection contains more than 80,000 works in all media. The Canadian collection is particularly impressive *(see pp20–21)*.

6 Textile Museum of Canada

MAP K3 ▪ 55 Centre Ave ▪ 416 599 5321 ▪ Open 11am–5pm daily (until 8pm Wed) ▪ Adm ▪ www.textilemuseum.ca

A permanent collection of over 10,000 fabrics, quilts, ceremonial cloths, and carpets from around the world are housed in this small but excellent museum. Temporary contemporary exhibits round out the historical artifacts.

7 Bata Shoe Museum

This unusual building, resembling a stylized shoebox, houses more than 13,000 artifacts, covering 4,500 years of footwear history. Artifacts represent an unparalleled range, from Ancient Egyptian funerary shoes (1500 BC) to 19th-century Nigerian camel-riding boots to Elvis Presley's patent blue loafers *(see p76)*.

8 Ontario Science Centre

Here, hundreds of interactive exhibits make science fascinating and fun. Youthful visitors can touch a tornado, navigate their way in a rocket chair, explore the hair-raising effects of electricity, send paper whooshing up a wind tunnel, and construct ramps and loops for balls to whiz around on *(see p95)*.

⑨ Aga Khan Museum

This architecturally stunning museum showcases the artistic and scientific heritage of Muslim civilizations from the Iberian Peninsula to China. Artifacts, dating from the 8th through the 21st centuries, include manuscripts, paintings, and ceramics. The museum auditorium hosts a varied cultural program through the year, and the public gardens are a tranquil spot for a break *(see p96)*.

Auditorium, Aga Khan Museum

⑩ Toronto Dominion Gallery of Inuit Art

Most of the 200 pieces in this gallery specializing in postwar Inuit sculpture are carved soapstone, each evocative of the landscape, culture, and legends of the indigenous people of Canada's harsh Arctic region. The gallery's design echoes that of the TD Bank Tower, by modernist architect Mies van der Rohe *(see p70)*.

The futuristic Ontario Science Centre

TOP 10 SMALL MUSEUMS

Visitors at Campbell House

1 St. Lawrence Market Gallery
This second-floor gallery has exhibits on art, culture, and history *(see p90)*.

2 Mackenzie House
The home of Toronto's first mayor *(see p87)*.

3 Toronto's First Post Office
A historic museum and working post office *(see p89)*.

4 TIFF Bell Lightbox
MAP J4 ▪ 350 King St W ▪ 416 599 8433 ▪ Open Tue–Sun ▪ Adm
Film-focused exhibitions at the HQ of the Toronto International Film Festival.

5 MOCCA
MAP B4 ▪ 952 Queen St W ▪ 416 395 0067 ▪ Open Tue–Sun
Innovative works by emerging artists.

6 Redpath Sugar Museum
MAP M6 ▪ 95 Queens Quay E ▪ 416 933 8341 ▪ Open Mon–Fri
Next door to a refinery, this museum tells the history of sugar production.

7 Campbell House
This is the oldest remaining building (1822) in the city *(see p77)*.

8 University of Toronto Art Centre
MAP J1 ▪ 15 King's College Circle ▪ 416 978 1838 ▪ Open Tue–Sat
The impressive art collection behind University College.

9 Design Exchange
Various areas of Canadian design are showcased in the Art Deco building that was once the Toronto Stock Exchange *(see p70)*.

10 CBC Museum
MAP J5 ▪ 250 Front St W ▪ 416 205 5574
Celebrates the people and programs of Canada's national broadcaster.

Architectural Highlights

University College, the founding college of the University of Toronto

① University of Toronto

Founded in 1827 as King's College, this institute has many stately, refined buildings, such as the Romanesque Revival-style University College *(see p78)*.

② Brookfield Place

MAP L5 ■ 181 Bay St

Spanish architect Santiago Calatrava designed the striking atrium of this 1990 office complex. Its steel-and-glass canopy creates enchanting patterns of light and shadow.

Glass arcade, Brookfield Place

③ CN Tower

Defining the skyline, Toronto's most recognizable architectural icon is also the tallest building in the Western Hemisphere *(see pp16–17)*.

④ Toronto-Dominion Centre

Two austere, perfectly proportioned towers and a single-story pavilion of glass and black metal are Toronto's only design by International Style architect Ludwig Mies van der Rohe (1886–1969). Completed in 1971, the complex spurred the skyscraper boom that gave birth to the city's financial district. Four more towers were later added *(see p68)*.

⑤ Royal Bank Plaza

MAP K4 ■ 200 Bay St

The 14,000 mirrored windows of the two towers (1977) are insulated with 24-karat gold. There is $70 worth of gold on each window, totalling some $1 million – money saved on heating.

⑥ The L Tower

MAP L5 ■ 22 The Esplanade

Set beside the Sony Centre *(see p50)*, this 58-story skyscraper of condos was designed by Daniel Libeskind. Its towering curve makes it the most elegant high-rise in the city.

7 Old City Hall

Now serving as a courthouse, this Richardsonian Romanesque building, completed in 1899, was designed by the architect responsible for many of Toronto's grandest historic buildings, E. J. Lennox. For the best view of its clock tower, look north up Bay Street *(see p78)*.

8 Sharpe Centre for Design

MAP J3 ▪ 100 McCaul St

Propped up on 100-ft (30-m) stilts, this addition to the Ontario College of Art and Design is playful and audacious. The two-story "tabletop" building connects to the main building via a sloping tunnel.

9 Union Station

MAP K5 ▪ 65 Front St W

The Great Hall of this 1920s monumental stone railroad station has an 88-ft- (27-m-) high vaulted ceiling *(see p17)*.

10 City Hall

Causing a significant stir in 1960s Toronto, the design of New City Hall is bold, daring, and unique. Finnish architect Viljo Revell's two curving towers seem to embrace the central domed structure between them. A sweeping public plaza out front, Nathan Phillips Square, is the symbolic heart of the city *(see p77)*.

The distinctive towers of City Hall

TOP 10 PUBLIC ART SITES

King Street exhibit: The Pasture

1 The Pasture
MAP L4 ▪ 77 King St W
Joe Fafard's seven bronze, life-size cows are in gentle repose.

2 Three Way Piece No. 2
MAP K3 ▪ Nathan Phillips Sq
Aka *The Archer*, this Henry Moore bronze, controversial when installed in 1966, is now a local favorite.

3 Immigrant Family
MAP L5 ▪ 18 Yonge St
This tomato-shaped family by sculptor Tom Otterness is thought-provoking.

4 Toronto Sculpture Garden
MAP L4 ▪ 115 King St E
Rotating exhibits of contemporary site-specific works.

5 Red Canoe
MAP H5 ▪ Canoe Landing Park
A huge canoe sits atop a mound with views over the Gardiner Expressway.

6 Search Light, Star Light, Spot Light
MAP K5 ▪ Air Canada Centre
Three hollow metal columns are pierced by hundreds of stars lit from within.

7 Mountain
MAP J4 ▪ Simcoe Park
This layered aluminum sculpture, cut with water jets, is by Anish Kapoor.

8 The Audience
MAP J5
"Fans" spill out of the Rogers Centre in this frieze by Michael Snow.

9 Woodpecker Column
MAP J5 ▪ 222 Bremner Blvd
Woodpeckers strike at this 100-ft (30-m) column.

10 City People
MAP K4 ▪ Royal Bank Plaza
Colorful figures spin softly in the breeze.

🔟 Green Spaces

1 High Park
Several miles of bicycle and walking trails meander through formal gardens, wooded ravines, and a rare oak savanna habitat in downtown's largest park. At the south end is Colborne Lodge and Grenadier Pond, where locals fish in summer and skate in winter (see p98).

High Park, downtown's green oasis

2 Mount Pleasant Cemetery
MAP D1

The beautiful array of trees – many magnificently old and stately – in this cemetery dating from 1876 qualifies it as a bona fide arboretum. A walk through the lovely grounds will reveal the graves of several notable Canadians, including pianist Glenn Gould (1932–82), whose marker is carved with the opening bars of Bach's *Goldberg Variations*.

3 Leslie Street Spit
MAP F6

This area is officially known as the Outer Harbour East Headland. The northern half, designated as a nature reserve, is a man-made peninsula extending 3 miles (5 km) into Lake Ontario. More than 290 bird species have been seen here, and its forests, wetlands, and meadows contain rare plants. A lighthouse at the southern tip is a popular cyclist's destination.

4 Edwards Gardens
Flowerbeds showcasing rhododendrons make this formal oasis very popular in summer, especially for wedding parties. The Teaching Garden lets kids learn hands-on about nature. The Toronto Botanical Garden (see p98), a horticultural center, is also here.

5 Yorkville Park
MAP C3

This gem packs a punch within its borders. It is divided into a series of gardens, each with a different theme, such as aspen grove, wetland, and meadow. Jets of mist rise at intervals around conifers; the enormous chunk of Canadian Shield granite makes a perfect perch for a rest.

6 Humber Bay Park East
MAP A2

Views of the city don't get much better than those from here. Easily accessible by bike on the Waterfront Trail, the park is also great for those on foot. A major habitat restoration, including wild flower meadow plantings, attracts birds and butterflies (see p98), while walkways and interpretive signs complement a series of stormwater cleansing ponds.

7 Toronto Music Garden
This is one of the city's most unusual gardens: each of its six sections is inspired by a movement of Bach's *First Suite for Unaccompanied Cello*. The swirling paths, hills, and groves are dazzling (see p67).

8 Evergreen Brick Works

Nature and a city park have reclaimed the quarry of this former brickworks: ponds and meadows of what is known as Weston Quarry Gardens attract birds and wildlife. Stop by the excavated "wall" to see the fossils of the area's early flora and fauna and its geologic history; some of the layers of deposits are over a million years old *(see p89)*.

9 Rouge National Urban Park

Spread across 31 sq miles (79 sq km) along the Rouge River, the park was designated a National Urban Park in 2011, the first of its kind in Canada. You can easily spend a day exploring its diversity of wildlife and plants, including a lakeside marsh *(see p98)*.

Chipmunk, Rouge National Urban Park

10 Ashbridges Bay Park
MAP B2

Enjoy a picnic at this lakeside park while watching boats, or play a game at the baseball diamond. At the north end, the Martin Goodman bike trail *(see p98)* meets the Beach boardwalk.

A path through Toronto Music Garden

TOP 10 SPECTATOR SPORTS

A Maple Leafs player at a game

1 Toronto Maple Leafs
MAP K5 ▪ Air Canada Centre, 40 Bay St ▪ 416 703 5323
This NHL team inspires adoration.

2 Toronto Blue Jays
MAP J5 ▪ Rogers Centre, 1 Blue Jays Way ▪ 1-888-OK-GO-JAY
Member of baseball's American League.

3 Toronto Raptors
MAP K5 ▪ Air Canada Centre, 40 Bay St ▪ 416 366 3865
Popular NBA team that delights fans.

4 Toronto Argonauts
MAP J5 ▪ Rogers Centre, 1 Blue Jays Way ▪ 416 341 2746
Canadian Football League team.

5 Toronto Rock
MAP K5 ▪ Air Canada Centre, 40 Bay St ▪ 416 596 3075
Players of lacrosse, the country's official national sport.

6 Toronto FC
MAP A5 ▪ BMO Field, Exhibition Place ▪ 416 360 4625
The city's Major League Soccer team.

7 Woodbine Race Track
MAP A1 ▪ 555 Rexdale Blvd ▪ 416 675 7223
Home of the Queen's Plate horse race.

8 Honda Indy
MAP A5 ▪ 416 588 7223
Canadian highlight of the IZOD Indy Car racing series at Exhibition Place.

9 Scotiabank Toronto Waterfront Marathon
MAP A5–F5 ▪ 416 944 2765
Boston Marathon qualifier along the shore and through the Don Valley.

10 Toronto Marlies
MAP A5 ▪ Ricoh Coliseum, Exhibition Place ▪ 416 597 7825
This AHL team sends players to the NHL.

�__TOP10__ Off the Beaten Path

1 The Haunted Walk
www.hauntedwalk.com/
toronto-tours

This is a 90-minute walking tour of Toronto's darker past. Guides are local storytellers and amateur historians who share tales of ghostly encounters in downtown Toronto.

2 Graffiti Alley
MAP H4 ■ Enter at 753 Queen St W

South of Chinatown (see p77), Graffiti Alley is actually a series of connected alleyways. As the name suggests, it

Colorful street art, Graffiti Alley

is an urban canvas of vibrant street art created by talented local artists and used in many fashion shoots. It is best to go during daylight hours.

3 The Junction
MAP A2 ■ 20 Jerome St

In 1904, the residents of what was then a suburb voted to ban the sale of alcohol. The area remained dry until 1996. Today, at the corner of Dundas West and Keele Street, four century-old buildings rise from the ground. Head here for a mix of old and new, with chic bars, restaurants, shops, and a terracotta house.

4 Jarvis Street Mansions
MAP M1 ■ Jarvis St

To see where Toronto's superrich once lived, check out the remaining grand homes along Jarvis Street. The Massey family (owners of a farm-equipment empire) called No. 515 home. Now a restaurant in the Keg chain, it is a designated heritage property, along with No. 519 Jarvis and two buildings on Wellesley Place.

5 Wychwood Park
MAP B1 ■ Entrance between 77 and 81 Alcina Ave

This late 19th-century enclave of gracious homes and tree-lined streets is a village within a big city. Founded as an artist's colony, it is now a private community managed by local residents. The public can enter through a little-known pedestrian passageway and wander through the grounds.

6 Toronto Necropolis

MAP E3 ■ 200 Winchester St, near Riverdale Farm

The Necropolis is the resting place of many of Toronto's famous citizens, including William Lyon Mackenzie, first mayor of Toronto and a leader of the Upper Canada Rebellion. The non-sectarian Gothic chapel is tranquil, and rare shrubs and Victorian monuments line the pathways.

7 Humber Bay Arch Bridge and Sheldon Lookout

MAP A2 ■ Martin Goodman Trail, south of Lakeshore Bvd W and near Windermere Ave

This arched pedestrian bridge sits at the mouth of the Humber River. Originally the start of an ancient First Nations trading route, it still features decorations that reflect the city's Native heritage. The bridge and the Sheldon Lookout to the west afford spectacular views of the city.

8 Pacific Mall

MAP B1 ■ 4300 Steeles Ave E ■ 905 470 8785

A wonderful slice of Asia in Toronto, Pacific Mall is said to be the largest indoor Chinese shopping center in North America. At the northeast end of the city, it stocks everything from electronics to hand-pulled noodles.

BAPS Shri Swaminarayan Mandir

9 Guild Park

MAP B1 ■ 201 Guildwood Parkway ■ www.todocanada.ca/city/toronto/listing/guildwood-park-gardens-scarborough-ontario

Toronto's most beloved architectural ruins lie at Guild Park, including old bank facades and columns, a school belfry, and other fragments of the city's rich architectural history. The park is located along the breathtaking Scarborough Bluffs.

Ancient ruins dotting Guild Park

10 BAPS Shri Swaminarayan Mandir

MAP A1 ■ 61 Claireville Dr ■ 416 798 2277 ■ www.baps.org

The BAPS Shri Swaminarayan Mandir is a traditional Hindu place of worship – and an architectural masterpiece set in a nondescript industrial location. It is made of 24,000 pieces of hand-sculpted Italian marble, and its extensive grounds include a Heritage Museum that is open to visitors.

Children's Attractions

1 Ripley's Aquarium of Canada

Children will love the huge tanks filled with all things marine, especially the ones that have perspex bubbles and tunnels they can crawl into to be part of the display *(see pp28–9)*.

2 Hockey Hall of Fame

Budding hockey stars can test their skill whacking pucks and guarding goal at this shrine to the sport, which houses more hockey memorabilia than you can shake a stick at *(see pp32–3)*.

Logo from the Hockey Hall of Fame

3 Ontario Science Centre

There will be no need to rein in the kids at this science-based learning playground. Instead, you can let them charge through more than 800 hands-on exhibits encompassing everything from sports to medicine, and computers to electricity *(see p95)*.

4 Harbourfront Centre

The kid-friendly attractions and events at this lakefront center ensure it's always busy. Children especially love watching artisans at work in the Artport's Craft Studio, the ice-skating rink, and open-air concerts *(see p67)*.

5 Young People's Theatre

This theater presents excellent productions that are always a hit with kids. The facade of the original building, built in 1881 as a stable for streetcar-pulling horses, can still be seen *(see p71)*.

6 Centre Island

A major highlight of this Toronto Island is Centreville *(see p19)*, a bustling amusement park. Some 30 old-fashioned rides include swan-shaped paddle boats, a lovely 1907 carousel, and even pony rides.

7 Canada's Wonderland

This amusement park has 200 attractions, including over 69 rides, a water park, and live shows. There are plenty of thrilling rides for older kids, including one of the world's tallest roller coasters, Leviathan. Little ones will love the tamer rides, including a tug boat *(see p95)*.

Families having fun riding the Funway at Canada's Wonderland

Kids admiring a snake, Toronto Zoo

8 Toronto Zoo

Exhibiting animals in their natural habitats is the policy of this zoo, which aims for meaningful education rather than theme-park spectacle. Six geographic areas are represented in pavilions filled with over 500 species, and large outdoor enclosures allow animals to roam freely (see p95).

9 Riverdale Farm

MAP E3 ▪ 201 Winchester St
▪ Open 9am–5pm daily

This agricultural education center and working farm in the middle of the city is home to many barnyard favorites – pigs, goats, sheep, horses, and chickens. Its post-and-beam barns date from the 19th century. This is a re-creation of a working farm, and animals should not be petted.

10 Royal Ontario Museum

Canada's largest museum is a truly magical place for children. It makes a special effort to have plenty of hands-on exhibits: the Dinosaur Gallery and mummy cases are strictly "don't touch," but the Hands-On Biodiversity Gallery will enchant youngsters with its fun, interactive exhibits, as will the CIBC Discovery Room (see pp12–15).

TOP 10 PLACES TO EAT WITH KIDS

1 Sunset Grill
MAP J4 ▪ 2006 Queen St E, The Beach ▪ 416 690 9985
Children love diners, and this is a particularly good one.

2 Wayne Gretzky's
MAP J4 ▪ 99 Blue Jays Way
▪ 416 979 7825
Pub fare and hockey memorabilia.

3 Five Doors North
MAP B2 ▪ 2088 Yonge St
▪ 416 480 6234
Classic Italian pastas and grilled meats.

4 Swiss Chalet
MAP J6 ▪ 266 Queens Quay W
▪ 416 596 7292
Canadian chain stuck in the 1980s, but reliably kid pleasing.

5 Stack
Dependable BBQ restaurant with mini portions for children (see p99).

6 Magic Oven
MAP F3 ▪ 798 Danforth Ave
▪ 416 868 6836
Delicious pizza and pasta east of Pape.

7 Lakeview Restaurant
MAP A4 ▪ 1123 Dundas St W
▪ 416 535 2828
Old-style diner with retro menu.

8 La Cubana
MAP A2 ▪ 392 Roncesvalles Ave
▪ 416 538 7500
Familiy-friendly with a great patio.

9 Fancy Franks Gourmet Hot Dogs
MAP H2 ▪ 326 College St ▪ 416 920 3647
Wiener shop offering 18 signature all-beef hot dogs.

10 Old Spaghetti Factory
MAP L5 ▪ 54 The Esplanade
▪ 416 864 9761
A perennial favorite, great for groups.

Old Spaghetti Factory

🔟 Entertainment Venues

The spectacularly preserved auditorium at the Elgin Theatre

1 Elgin and Winter Garden Theatres

These two theaters have been restored to their original splendor. Opened in 1913 as a double-decker venue – with the Winter Garden seven stories above the Elgin – they host concerts, operas, and hit Broadway musicals *(see p71)*.

2 Koerner Hall

MAP C3 ■ 273 Bloor St W ■ 416 408 0208 ■ www.performance. rcmusica.ca

Part of the Royal Conservatory of Music's Telus Centre for Performing and Learning, Koerner Hall's acoustics are second to none. Enjoy jazz, classical, and World Music here.

3 Sony Centre for the Performing Arts

MAP L5 ■ 1 Front St E ■ 1 855 872 7669 ■ www.sonycentre.ca

Famed dancer Mikhail Baryshnikov defected here from the Soviet Union in 1979. The now-refurbished theater mounts shows as diverse as Beck, Sesame Street Live, and the Eifman St. Petersburg Ballet.

4 Molson Amphitheatre

MAP A5 ■ 909 Lake Shore Blvd W ■ 416 260 5600 ■ www.canadian amphitheatre.net

With its lakeside setting, this is a great place for a summer concert. There's seating for 8,000 under the canopy, plus space for 8,000 more on the grass.

5 Toronto Centre for the Arts

MAP A1 ■ 5040 Yonge St ■ 416 250 3708 ■ www.tocentre.com

In surburban North York, the center's four stages host Broadway musicals, symphony orchestras, and well-known popular and classical singers.

6 Roy Thomson Hall

MAP J4 ■ 60 Simcoe St ■ 416 872 4255 ■ www.roythomson.com

This concert hall's innovative design ensures that everyone in the audience is within 100 ft (30 m) of the stage.

Music performance at Koerner Hall

(7) St. Lawrence Centre for the Arts

MAP L5 ■ 27 Front St E ■ 416 366 7723 ■ www.stlc.com

This venue presents theater, dance, and music, as well as lectures on subjects of topical interest, in its two intimate spaces – the larger Bluma Appel Theatre, and the Jane Mallet Theatre, which features recitals and performances by groups such as the Toronto Operetta Theatre Company.

(8) Young Centre for the Performing Arts

MAP E5 ■ 50 Tank House Lane ■ 416 866 8666 ■ www.youngcentre.ca

The performance space here is also the main venue for the George Brown Theatre School. It hosts a number of other local performances.

Four Seasons Centre lit up at night

(9) Four Seasons Centre for the Performing Arts

MAP K4 ■ 145 Queen St W ■ COC: 416 363 8231, www.coc.ca ■ NBC: 416 345 9595, www.national.ballet.ca

This large, beautiful space is home to two of Canada's most important performing arts companies – the Canadian Opera Company and the National Ballet of Canada.

(10) Massey Hall

MAP L4 ■ 178 Victoria St ■ 416 872 4255 ■ www.masseyhall.com

This grande dame opened in 1894. Its 2,750 seats and superb acoustics provide a surprisingly intimate setting for jazz, blues, and folk shows.

TOP 10 PERFORMING ARTS GROUPS

National Ballet of Canada

1 Canadian Opera Company
MAP K4 ■ www.coc.ca
Largest producer of opera in Canada with seven productions each season.

2 Tarragon Theatre
MAP B2 ■ www.tarragontheatre.com
Performances of new innovative works by Canadian playwrights.

3 Tafelmusik
MAP C3 ■ www.tafelmusik.org
The ensemble plays Baroque chamber music on period instruments.

4 Theatre Passe Muraille
MAP G3 ■ passemuraille.ca
Pioneers that have helped shape a distinctly Canadian voice (see p71).

5 Toronto Mendelssohn Choir
MAP B3 ■ www.tmchoir.org
Canada's oldest vocal ensemble presented its first concert in 1895.

6 Toronto Symphony Orchestra
MAP J4 ■ www.tso.ca
This renowned orchestra delights with the classics at the Roy Thomson Hall.

7 Canadian Stage
MAP E5 ■ www.canadianstage.com
Productions of international and Canadian works, including musicals.

8 National Ballet of Canada
MAP K4 ■ national.ballet.ca
Internationally acclaimed company with the classics and new productions.

9 Toronto Dance Theatre
MAP E3 ■ www.tdt.org
Intelligent and visually striking modern dance by an influential dance troupe.

10 Soulpepper Theatre Company
MAP E5 ■ www.soulpepper.ca
Interesting Canadian interpretations of international classics.

Gay and Lesbian Hangouts

1 Club 120
MAP L4 ■ 120 Church St
■ www.club120.ca

Over two floors above a restaurant on the intersection of Church and Richmond streets, this upscale nightclub hosts a plethora of events, including T-Girl nights, open-mic comedy, and a monthly naked dance party TNT!MEN. On the weekends the crowds mix up and things get going with international DJs holding court late into the night. Check the website for the events schedule.

2 Barbara Hall Park
MAP L1 ■ 519 Church St

This popular meeting place, with its benches and greenery, is home to a permanent AIDS memorial, installed in 1993. The pillars are inscribed, upon request and with no geographic restrictions, with the names of those lost to the virus. The Universal Remembrance Plaque is a tribute to those who remain unnamed.

AIDS memorial, Barbara Hall Park

3 Woody's
MAP L1 ■ 467 Church St ■ 416 972 0887

A stuffed rhinoceros head presiding over the bar greets patrons at this local watering hole. A pool table and soft-core videos keep the clientele entertained, as do special events, such as the Best Chest contest, here and at sibling bar Sailor, next door.

Neon-illuminated Glad Day Bookshop

4 Glad Day Bookshop
MAP L1 ■ 499 Church St
■ 416 961 4161

Established in 1970 as Canada's first gay and lesbian bookstore, Glad Day's excellent collection includes a wide selection of academic, fiction, and hard-to-find titles, as well as racy picture books and magazines. The used books section on the second floor is worth checking out.

5 Crews & Tangos
MAP L1 ■ 508 Church St
■ 637 349 7469

This is a fun spot to dance the night away to hip hop, R&B, top-40 hits, and the best local and NY-based DJs around. The crowd is mixed and welcoming. If you are after some theatricality, then this is the right place – they host a popular drag show every night.

6 Church Street
MAP L1

The intersection of Church and Wellesley streets is the epicenter of Toronto's gay village and has been home to a large gay and lesbian community for decades. Excellent bars, restaurants, and specialty shops make the strip a great place to soak up the scene, as leathermen, muscle boys, and drag queens strut their stuff. The 519 Community Centre hosts regular social events and gatherings, as well as offering a multitude of drop-in programs and short-term counseling.

7 The Beaver
MAP A4 ■ 1192 Queen St W
■ 416 537 2768

Head to this laid-back little café that turns into raucous fun from 11pm, featuring DJs that spin dancehall, hip hop, 1990s grunge, and even country. There's karaoke on Sundays.

8 Hair of the Dog
MAP L2 ■ 425 Church St
■ 416 964 2708

A laid-back spot serving standard pub fare alongside draft beer. The sizeable patio, located at the back and south facing, is the big draw here.

9 Hanlan's Point Beach
MAP B6

This secluded Toronto Island beach has the city's only official clothing-optional area (don't take off your clothes until you reach the fenced section at the south end). In 1999, it reclaimed its status as a nude beach, as it was between 1894 and 1930, enabling nudists and cruisers to again bathe in the buff. There are "no swimming" signs when water pollution levels are high *(see p19)*.

10 Buddies in Bad Times Theatre
MAP L1 ■ 12 Alexander St ■ 416 975 8555 ■ www.buddiesinbadtimes.com

This groundbreaking company, established in 1979, is the city's oldest and largest venue for queer-culture productions. Renowned for innovative, edgy works, productions often push the boundaries of artistic convention and sometimes even propriety. On Saturdays at 10:30pm Tallulah's Cabaret takes over with DJs and wild dancing and, true to its name, some kind of outrageous performance. There's plenty of information on Tallulah's Cabaret nights, plus upcoming festivals and events, on the theater's website, where you can also buy tickets.

Buddies in Bad Times Theatre

Restaurants

1 Mildred's Temple Kitchen

Set in a post-industrial district of Victorian-era brick factories, Mildred's features a farmhouse chic menu of dishes created with seasonal produce. On weekends try the Big Brunch Skillet of pulled pork, black beans, and eggs, or Veda's Choice (eggs Benedict on a croissant). The rosemary bacon is cured in-house *(see p83)*.

2 Lady Marmalade

Among the best places for brunch in breakfast-crazy Leslieville. Mexican-inspired *huevos* and creative takes on eggs Benedict *(see p93)*.

3 Le Sélect Bistro

A much-loved Toronto mainstay with cane chairs on the patio, a striped awning, and a proper zinc bar. It serves all the popular weekend brunch options, Alsace classics including *choucroute,* as well as French favorites such as steak tartare, gigot d'agneau, and confit de canard that are prepared with regional ingredients *(see p73)*.

4 Chiado

Dine on the freshest fish and seafood to be had in the city, flown in from the world's wharfs daily and transformed into the most luxurious of Portuguese fare. The wine list is replete with unusual offerings, which the waitstaff are expert at elucidating and pairing with dishes. Try the tapas menu at the wine bar in the restaurant's modern annex addition, Senhor Antonio *(see p99)*.

Blueberry pancakes, Aunties and Uncles

5 Aunties and Uncles

This is a charmingly eclectic eatery housed in a former 1950s barber shop. The soups, salads, omelets, and sandwiches here are excellent, and the juice is freshly squeezed. Almost everything is served with trademark sides of pea meal bacon and buttery challah toast *(see p83)*.

6 Lai Wah Heen

Serving exceptional Cantonese cuisine, this elegant two-level restaurant in the DoubleTree by Hilton redefines classic Chinese fare. Elegant details include silver chopstick rests and starched linens on the round tables, which are suitable for large groups and conducive to sharing (smaller tables also available). The Sunday dim sum is particularly popular *(see p83)*.

French-style chic, Le Sélect Bistro

Contemporary setting at the Chase

7 The Chase

Refined dining is on offer in a bright, window-walled penthouse atop the Heritage listed Dineen Building. Carefully prepared dishes, such as lobster layered with truffles or chestnut and foie gras ravioli, allow the world-class food to sing. There's less formal dining in The Chase Fish and Oyster on the ground floor.

8 Canoe

Stellar views from the 54th floor of the Toronto Dominion Bank Tower make this one of the most enchanting eateries in the city. Lunchtime business crowds close deals over lobster club sandwiches on brioche, but the evening ambience is more romantic. Menu mainstays include Canadian elk and Quebec suckling pig (see p73).

9 Noce

This intimate restaurant serves marvelous Italian food, delivered with welcoming, friendly service. The homemade pasta specials are always superb, as are grilled and roasted meats. The summer patio is great for al fresco dining (see p83).

10 Buca

This trendy basement *osteria* is tucked up an alleyway beside the Scholastic building. The acclaimed, earthy Italian menu is based on the "nose-to-tail" philosophy of utilizing the entire animal in cooking. Fare includes unusual quirks such as bison prosciutto (see p73).

TOP 10 BEST CANADIAN SNACKS

1 Chinese Buns
Steamed dough filled with savory meat, vegetables, or sweet coconut and red bean paste. Eat piping hot.

2 Poutine
Hailing from Québec, *poutine* (french fries topped with cheese curds and hot gravy) is now ubiquitous in Toronto.

3 Falafel
Deep-fried chickpea balls in pita pockets stuffed with *tahini* sauce, onion, and tomato.

4 Bubble Tea
An Asian concoction of sweet, flavored cold tea, milk, and tapioca pearls.

5 Gelato
More refreshing and lighter than ice cream, Italian ices come in a range of flavors, from lemon to caramel.

6 Corn on the Cob
Little India street vendors prepare grilled corn glazed with lemon juice and tangy spices.

7 Hot Dogs
Ubiquitous outdoor carts grill hot dogs, veggie dogs, and sausages. Polish sausage is a favorite, piled high with all the fixings – pickles, hot mustard, and sauerkraut.

8 Jamaican Roti
Soft flat bread encases a variety of fillings, from curried goat or chicken to spinach and squash. The hot sauce is optional.

9 Churrasco Chicken
Spiked with tangy Portuguese *piri piri* sauce, then barbecued to perfection; served on a bun or with roasted spuds.

10 Roasted Chestnuts
Sidewalk vendors sell steaming-hot smoky-flavored roast chestnuts in summer and fall.

Chinese steamed buns

For a key to restaurant price ranges see p73

🔟 Bars and Clubs

A live band entertaining an audience at the Lula Lounge

1 Lula Lounge

Lively bands and hot DJs play everything Latin, from merengue to salsa. Enjoy dinner before the show, arrive later for drinks, or go all out with a dance lesson/dinner show package *(see p81)*.

2 The Bar at ALO

This classic bar – all polished brass and gracious staff – is on the third floor of a Victorian building. The food is several cuts above the usual, with small plates of dishes such as sashimi or rack of pork. Cocktails (try the Armagnac old-fashioned) are served up with panache *(see p83)*.

The Bar at ALO with a range of drinks

3 Bar Hop

The bars that sold proper cask-pulled beer were few and far between a decade ago, but Toronto has finally joined the craft beer renaissance. Bar Hop is among the best, regularly bringing in guest beers to join its 36 taps *(see p72)*.

4 d|bar

It's all about style at this busy see-and-be-seen bar on the first floor of the prestigious Four Seasons Hotel in fashionable Yorkville. Adept servers prepare the perfect cocktail in a miniature shaker at your table; nary a drop is spilled. At the bar, business tycoons talk takeovers while scoping out the room *(see p81)*.

5 Pravda Vodka House

Decked out in gold and red Russian furnishings, with portraits of Stalin and Lenin on the walls, this bar serves up more than 70 of the world's best vodkas *(see p92)*.

6 The Fifth Social Club

The loft-style dance club of this restaurant/bar venue caters to the 25-plus crowd. Bouncers ignore the jeans-clad in favor of those in casual-smart attire. Inside, grab a drink at one of four bars, then dance to R&B and top-40 music *(see p72)*.

7 Cameron House

Giant "ants" on the front of this former flophouse signal a different bar experience. Notable for the acts that played here before making it big, this low-key bar is dedicated to up-and-coming musicians. Join foot-stomping regulars on weekends for pay-what-you-can country music (see p81).

8 The Roof Lounge

A haunt of creative types, this bar atop the Park Hyatt Hotel offers refuge from daily stresses. In winter, a fireplace and huge leather chairs beckon; in summer, spectacular views from the terrace (see p81).

9 Irish Embassy Pub & Grill

Pub lovers will feel at home with the mahogany bar, and the stool and booth seating set among the marble columns of this historic bank building. Good choice of beers on tap, and tasty pub food (see p72).

Irish Embassy Pub & Grill

10 Bar at Canoe

On the 54th floor of the TD Bank Tower (see p68), this sophisticated spot caters to corporate wheelers and dealers (reduced to size against the magnificent view of Lake Ontario). There's an excellent selection of wines, cocktails, and beers. Note that the bar is closed on weekends (see p72).

TOP 10 VENUES FOR LIVE MUSIC

Mood lighting at Adelaide Hall

1 Opera House
MAP F4 ▪ 735 Queen St E
An eclectic range of bands plays beneath the ornate proscenium arch. All-ages shows and blues nights pack the place.

2 Rivoli
MAP H4 ▪ 334 Queen St W
Booking top alternative rock bands has made this spot a Toronto landmark.

3 Danforth Music Hall
MAP F3 ▪ 147 Danforth Ave
Originally a cinema, this mid-size venue has a balcony and slanted floors.

4 Horseshoe Tavern
MAP H4 ▪ 368 Queen St W
A stalwart of Queen West since 1947, showcasing the best of Toronto bands.

5 Adelaide Hall
MAP J4 ▪ 250 Adelaide St W
Great intimate venue for indie bands and other acts, in the heart of the city.

6 The Rex Hotel
MAP J3 ▪ 194 Queen St W
The hotel's jazz and blues bar attracts Canada's finest musicians.

7 Hugh's Room
MAP A4 ▪ 2261 Dundas St W
Enjoy a range of musical genres in a wonderfully intimate space.

8 Lee's Palace
MAP B3 ▪ 529 Bloor St W
This gritty joint hosts edgy rock bands.

9 Reservoir Lounge
MAP L4 ▪ 52 Wellington St E
Swing-jazz, jump blues, and southern fusion cuisine. Closed Sunday.

10 Phoenix Concert Theatre
MAP M1 ▪ 410 Sherbourne St
Rock bands, and dancing on DJ theme nights.

Shopping Destinations

1 Distillery Historic District

If you're looking for art or unique crafts visit the cobbled lanes of this enclave. More and more clothes retailers, including Canadian fashion heroes Gotstyle and cobbler John Fluevog, are moving into the area's stunning spaces (see pp26–7).

Indoor vendor, St. Lawrence Market

2 St. Lawrence Market

Considered by gastronomes around the globe to be one of the world's best markets, this is reason enough for food lovers to travel to Toronto. A huge selection of meat, fish, cheese, and produce, as well as hand-crafted gifts, make for a one-of-a-kind experience. Vendors pushing food samples and buskers add to the dynamic atmosphere; frequent special events and festivals liven things up even more. The market consists of the South and North (under redevelopment) buildings (see p88).

3 Bloor Street

Between Yonge Street and Avenue Road, Bloor Street grows ever more luxurious with branches of Hermès, Chanel, and Max Mara, as well as excellent homegrown stores. Drop by fine jewelers Birks; David's, one of the most glamorous shoe stores in the city; Holt Renfrew, a small department store specializing in high-end clothing; Harry Rosen, a superb men's clothing store with impeccable service; and the Roots flagship store, offering quality leather and sportswear (see p78).

4 Kensington Market

This chaotic enclave was once a Jewish market, but the dominant ethnic flavor is now Portuguese and West Indian, with hints of Asian and Hispanic. Reflecting this are the food shops, stocked with pulses, cassava, salted cod, cornbread, cheese, and spices. There are also gourmet butchers and delicatessens. Strains of Reggae and the waft of incense will lead you to the dimly lit secondhand clothing stores in the Victorian houses on Kensington Avenue (see p75).

Victorian houses at Kensington Market

Stores at the upscale Eaton Centre

5 CF Toronto Eaton Centre

Anchored at the southern end of Queen Street by Hudson's Bay and at the northern end by Nordstrom, this shopping oasis has something for every taste and budget – the range of goods across hundreds of stores is huge *(see pp30–31)*.

6 Chinatown

You may think you're in Hong Kong as you browse along Spadina Avenue and Dundas Street, speculating on the use of exotic ingredients such as dried shrimp and the odoriferous durian fruit, or eyeing the dizzying array of Chinese house-wares, knick-knacks, and herbal medicines on offer here *(see p77)*.

7 Queen Street West

MAP G4–J4

Artists after cheap rent settled among the textile shops along Queen Street between University Avenue and Bathurst Street in the early 1980s. Things have changed, and now the strip between John Street and Spadina is dominated by global brands including Gap and Zara. If you are after sneakers, there's plenty of choice, and the Crocs flagship store is here too.

8 West Queen West

For independent designs and trendy togs, Queen West of Bathurst is the place to head. You'll find great shoe shops with the latest designs, slick homewares, one-of-a-kind boutiques, and cafés galore. Cool international outlets have cropped up around Ossington, including Fred Perry and Stüssy *(see p80)*.

9 Leslieville

MAP F4

Lovers of vintage clothes, radios and vinyl, and mid-20th-century modern furniture will have a shopping fest along this eclectic stretch running between Logan and Greenwood. The shops are well spread out, with the greatest concentration being between Carlaw and Jones.

10 Yorkville

Clustered in this upscale district, choice boutiques and fine art galleries offer everything the well-heeled and monied traveler desires. The eclectic mix of independent shops is a welcome relief from the rows of brash luxury shops lining the southern edge of Yorkville *(see p79)*.

⑩ Toronto for Free

Entrance to the Thomas Fisher Library

① Unusual Libraries
Thomas Fisher Library: MAP J1; 120 St. George St; 416 978 5285 ■ Merril Collection of Science Fiction, Speculation & Fantasy: MAP H2; 239 College St; 416 393 7748

Part of the University of Toronto but open to the public, the Thomas Fisher Rare Book Library houses around 700,000 volumes. The Merril Collection is intriguing, offering more than 70,000 books in categories such as parapsychology and UFOs.

② Visit the Legislature
Tours: www.discoveryportal. ontla.on.ca

Toronto is the capital of Ontario, and visitors can take a variety of free tours (from 8:30am to 4:30pm most days) that provide glimpses into the province's Parliament. Themes include the Legislature's history and the architecture of the historic building that houses it (see p78).

Ice skating at Nathan Phillips Square

③ Improv Comedy
Second City Toronto: MAP J4; 51 Mercer St; 416 343 0011; www. secondcity.com

Free Second City improv comedy takes place at least 4 days a week; check online for details. The set happens after the main revue (which you don't have to attend) and runs for about 30–45 minutes.

④ Walking Tours
Tour Guys: www.tourguys.ca/ toronto ■ Heritage Canada: www. heritagetoronto.org/programs/tours

Tour Guys offers several free walking tours of Toronto, with themes such as history, food, and graffiti. To learn more about Toronto's architectural heritage try one of the free tours offered by Heritage Canada.

⑤ Ice Skating in Winter
MAP K3 ■ nathanphillips squareskaterentals.com

During winter, the reflecting pool in Nathan Phillips Square becomes a popular ice-skating rink. Visitors without skates of their own can rent a pair on site for a small fee.

⑥ Concerts
Canadian Opera Company: www.coc.ca/performancesandtickets/ freeconcertseries.aspx

The COC offers free indoor concerts most Tuesdays and Thursdays (Sep–Jun), with occasional performances on Wednesdays. Free outdoor performances take place in summer.

7 Watch a Movie Being Made

ACTRA Toronto: www.actratoronto.com/whats-shooting

ACTRA lists the major productions currently being filmed on location in the city, so visitors can head down and experience the making of a major motion picture firsthand.

8 Museums and Galleries

CBC Museum at the CBC Broadcasting Centre: MAP J5; 250 Front St W; www.cbc.ca/museum

Many museums, such as the Aga Khan Museum *(see p96)*, offer free entry at certain times. For a peek into Canadian culture, try the CBC Museum, with interactive exhibits on well-known Canadian programs.

Gallery at the Aga Khan Museum

9 Live Studio Audiences

CBC Broadcasting Centre: MAP J5; 250 Front St W; cbchelp.cbc.ca

Information on the popular CBC programs that allow visitors to be part of a live studio audience for free can be found on the CBC website. Advance booking is key.

10 Summer Outdoor Films

City Cinema: MAP L3; Yonge-Dundas Sq; www.ydsquare.ca/city-cinema.html ■ Free Flicks: MAP J6; Harbourfront; www.harbourfrontcentre.com/freeflicks09/index.cfm

Toronto loves its cinema, with plenty of free film showings to be found in the city. City Cinema offers free films (mostly frothy comedies) on Tuesdays at sunset. For crowd-pleasing movies, try Free Flicks at Harbourfront on Wednesdays at dusk.

TOP 10 BUDGET TIPS

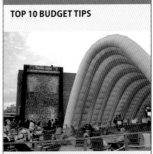

Summer waterfront festival

1 CityPass gives substantial discounts to the collection of attractions that are featured (www.citypass.com/toronto). This booklet is valid for 9 consecutive days, starting from the first day that you use it.

2 Throughout summer, a multitude of free events, such as concerts, food festivals, and dancing on the pier, are held at Harbourfront *(see p67)*.

3 Buy a day pass from a subway boot if you're planning on making multiple trips; they offer real savings.

4 Several parks and beaches offer outdoor gyms, as well as grills and picnic tables (www.toronto.ca.parks).

5 Many hotels offer discounts when booked online. Members of auto clubs and AARP (American Association of Retired Persons) often get discounts.

6 Buffet lunches are popular and provide good value. At Dhaba Indian buffet (309 King Street West) there are more than 60 items to choose from for less than $15.

7 The city's board-game cafés, such as Snakes and Lattés (600 Bloor Street W) and C'est What (67 Front Street E), offer plenty of old-fashioned fun for around $5.

8 Tourism Toronto usually has good deals on packages for short stays throughout the year (www.seetorontonow.com).

9 Toronto Islands provide a relaxing day's entertainment for the cost of a ferry ride *(see pp18–19)*.

10 The Travellers' Aid booth in Union Station can provide details on good budget accommodations.

🔟 Festivals

An enthusiastic crowd being entertained at North By Northeast (NXNE)

① Hot Docs
Late Apr ■ www.hotdocs.ca

This 11-day festival is dedicated to the art of documentary film-making, with around 200 films from Canada and across the world screened in 16 venues across the city.

② Contact
May ■ www.scotiabank
contactphoto.com

The largest festival dedicated to photography in the world, Contact brings together over 1,500 artists to exhibit at 175 venues in the city. Big names round out the program along with retrospectives of the greats.

③ Luminato
Jun ■ www.luminato
festival.com

This internationally acclaimed multi-arts festival takes place over 10 days and brings out the cutting-edge big hitters – think Rufus Wainwright recreating Judy Garland's 1961 Carnegie Hall show. The festival offers music galore, both local and international, as well as dance performances and talks by the likes of musicians David Byrne, Joni Mitchell, and Buffy Sainte-Marie. There are also many free events and even some stuff for kids.

④ NXNE
Jun ■ www.nxne.com

It began as a grungy music event, but North By Northeast is now a cultural extravaganza encompassing film, art, talks, and new technology, and it takes over the downtown core for 10 days. Get your wristband and get out there – it's still an unbeatable chance to discover new bands.

⑤ Pride Week
Late Jun ■ www.pridetoronto.com

Toronto's Pride celebrations are legendary. Performances, music, and parties take over the Village around Church and Wellesley for 10 days. Three parades make sure all are represented – the Dyke March, Trans Parade, and the Pride Parade.

Revelers during Pride Week

6 Caribbean Carnival
Jul to early Aug ▪ www.torontocaribbean carnival.com

This three-week extravaganza celebrates all things Caribbean. The revelry culminates on the August long weekend with a huge parade, packed with elaborate costumes, along Lakeshore Boulevard.

7 Beaches International Jazz Festival
Late Jul ▪ www.beachesjazz.com

A free festival with mostly Canadian headliners, a Big Band Stage, and a Latino Stage. Over 40 bands play along Queen East – the crowds bring the neighborhood to a standstill.

8 SummerWorks
Aug ▪ www.summer works.ca

This 10-day festival of performance is run by SummerWorks, known for forward-thinking Canadian theater. It is Canada's biggest juried festival.

Actor Benedict Cumberbatch at TIFF

9 TIFF
Sep ▪ www.tiff.net

Showcasing over 300 films from as many as 60 countries, the Toronto International Film Festival draws stars, independent film-makers, and movie buffs to the city for 10 days in early September.

10 Nuit Blanche
Early Oct ▪ www.scotiabank nuitblanche.com

An all-night contemporary arts festival, with over 100 art events scattered across town. Stay up until dawn – it can get pretty interesting.

TOP 10 FAMILY EVENTS

1 Sugarbush Maple Syrup Festival
Mar–Apr ▪ www.maplesyrupfest.com
Learn how to make maple syrup.

2 TIFF Kids
Apr ▪ www.tiff.net
The best in contemporary and classic children's film.

3 Dragon Boat Race Festival
Jun ▪ www.dragonboats.com
Teams from around the world compete in a race at Centre Island.

4 Redpath Waterfront Festival
Jul ▪ www.towaterfrontfest.com
Fun along the shore: treasure hunts, a flyboarding competition, and dog trials.

5 Canada Day
Jul 1
Free concerts, activities, and fireworks at Mel Lastman Square.

6 Canadian National Exhibition
Mid-Aug to Labour Day (first Mon in Sep) ▪ www.theex.com
Themed pavilions, fairground amusements, and an air show.

7 Buskerfest
Sep ▪ www.torontobuskerfest.com
Acrobats, musicians, and lots more take over Yonge between Queen and College.

8 Word on the Street
Sep ▪ www.thewordonthestreet.ca
Literary festival with readings by popular authors.

9 Royal Agricultural Winter Fair
Nov ▪ www.royalfair.org
Country fair with horse jumping and livestock competitions.

10 Santa Claus Parade
Mid-Nov ▪ www.thesantaclaus parade.ca
Toronto tradition featuring marching bands, floats, and the big man himself.

Dragon Boat Race Festival

Toronto
Area by Area

Aerial view of the Toronto skyline with
the Toronto Islands in the foreground

🔟 Harbourfront and the Financial District

Harbourfront and the Financial District combine old and new in a vibrant mix. Along the shores of Lake Ontario, the origins of the city can be traced to the establishment of Fort York in 1793. As the town of York grew, spreading north, financial institutions settled around Bay and King streets. Skyscrapers and historic buildings are dotted throughout the area, while vaudeville theaters, restored to their original splendor, anchor an exuberant entertainment scene.

'The Audience' by Toronto artist Michael Snow, Rogers Centre

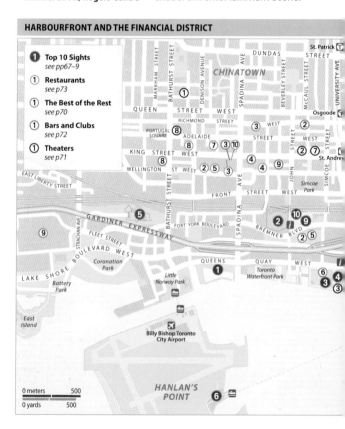

HARBOURFRONT AND THE FINANCIAL DISTRICT

① **Top 10 Sights**
see pp67–9

① **Restaurants**
see p73

① **The Best of the Rest**
see p70

① **Bars and Clubs**
see p72

① **Theaters**
see p71

Recital at the Toronto Music Garden

1 Toronto Music Garden
MAP H6 ■ 475 Queens Quay W
■ 416 973 4000 ■ www.harbourfront
centre.com/summermusic
This elegant garden, a collaboration
between famed cellist Yo Yo Ma,
landscape architect Julie Moir
Messervy, and city landscape archi-
tects, was inspired by Bach's *First
Suite for Unaccompanied Cello*. Each
movement in the suite – allemande,
courante, sarabande, menuets, and
gigue – plus a prelude, is represented by the plantings in one of the
six sections of the garden. Concerts
run from July through September.

2 Rogers Centre
MAP J5 ■ 1 Blue Jays Way
■ 416 341 1000
At the base of the CN Tower, this
sports and large-events venue is
home to the city's baseball team,
the Blue Jays, and football team, the
Argonauts. When built in 1989, it had
the world's only fully retractable roof
of its kind. When teams are not in
action, you can tour the facility.
Outside, a frieze by Toronto artist
Michael Snow depicts 14 spectators.

3 Harbourfront Centre
MAP K6 ■ 235 Queens Quay W
■ 416 973 4000 ■ Open 10am–11pm
Mon–Sat, 10am–9pm Sun ■ www.
harbourfrontcentre.com
This centre provides a diverse range
of recreational and cultural activities,
and the Bill Boyle Artport is its fulcrum.
Watch artists blowing glass in the
craft studios, or admire
the contemporary Can-
adian art at the Artport
Gallery. The Brigantine
Room hosts readings,
workshops, and theater
performances.

Harbourfront Centre

4 Queen's Quay Terminal
MAP K6 ▪ 207 Queens Quay W ▪ 416 203 3269 ▪ Open 10am–6pm daily

In a converted 1927 building, this is a mix of condos, offices, and a retail complex bursting with boutiques that sell unusual gift items. Good food is on offer at its restaurants, many with patios overlooking the water. Harbor cruises depart from the terminal.

Condos at Queen's Quay Terminal

5 Fort York
MAP G5 ▪ 250 Fort York Blvd ▪ 416 392 6907 ▪ Open early Sep–late May: 10am–4pm Mon–Fri, 10am–5pm Sat & Sun; late May–early Sep: 10am–5pm daily ▪ Closed for special events ▪ Adm

Established in 1793 to protect the growing city, this was the site of the Battle of York during the War of 1812, when the US invaded Upper Canada. The fort houses the country's largest collection of War of 1812 buildings, which display historic military items. Guides in costume give period music, musket, and drill demonstrations.

CANADA'S WAR AGAINST THE US

On June 18, 1812, the US declared war on Great Britain and, for many months, battled at various border outposts such as Detroit and Queenston Heights. In April 1813, American troops invaded and occupied York (as Toronto was then called), burning the Parliament and destroying much of Fort York. The US won the Battle of York, but they soon abandoned the town to fight battles in the Niagara Peninsula. The American war with Britain ended in stalemate on December 24, 1814, with the signing of the Treaty of Ghent.

6 Toronto Islands
Recreational opportunities abound on the car-free islands, from sunbathing and cycling to children's amusement rides. Ferries depart regularly for the islands from the foot of Bay Street; the 10-minute trip across the harbor offers unparalleled views of downtown (see pp18–19).

7 Toronto-Dominion Centre
MAP K4 ▪ 55 King St W

This six-tower complex is one of the most important pieces of architecture in the city (see p42). The black steel I-beams of the 1968 Toronto Dominion Bank Tower are trademark Mies van der Rohe (1886–1969), and perfectly reflect the famed architect's modernist dictum "Less is More." In the courtyard, seven bronze cow sculptures by Joe Fafard represent the roots of Canada's agrarian economy. Below ground is a shopping mall, the only one van der Rohe ever designed.

Canada Day at Fort York

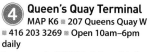

8 Hockey Hall of Fame

Hockey fans will be fascinated by the memorabilia in this museum dedicated to Canada's favorite sport. Everything from masks personalized by goalies to hand-carved skates from the 1840s reflect the history of the game. Have your photo taken with the iconic Stanley Cup, then test your skills at the game at the interactive exhibits (see pp32–3).

9 Ripley's Aquarium of Canada

This state-of-the-art aquarium at the base of the CN Tower features over 16,000 marine animals in 50 exhibits, with a capacity of 1.5 million US gallons (5.7 million liters) of water. The Dangerous Lagoon features three different types of shark and has North America's longest underwater viewing tunnel at 315 ft (96 m) (see pp28–9).

Viewing tunnel, Ripley's Aquarium

10 CN Tower

Soaring 1,815 ft (553 m) above downtown, this is the defining icon of the city's skyline and the tallest building in the Western Hemisphere. Check out the state-of-the-art theater showing short but thrilling 3-D movies, then let a glass-fronted elevator zip you, in less than a minute, up to one of four lookout levels. Access to the SkyPod, which costs extra, is via a separate elevator. The experience is vertiginous and tends to be rather cramped. The popular revolving 360 Restaurant, offers fine dining in serene surroundings (see pp16–17).

AN ART WALK

MORNING

Start at **Commerce Court North** (see p70) and admire the stunning lobby. Walk west along King Street, just past Bay Street and the TD Centre. Note the courtyard cows, part of Joe Fafard's sculpture *The Pasture* (see p43), on the lawn behind 77 King Street W. Just around the corner at 234 Bay Street is the **Design Exchange** (see p70), former home of the Toronto Stock Exchange. Admire the metallic Art Deco doors featuring icons representing industries from the 1930s, then head north up Bay Street to **Mercatto** (see p73) for an Italian lunch.

AFTERNOON

Zigzag your way to Simcoe Park, on Front Street west of Simcoe, and admire the Anish Kapoor sculpture *Mountain* (see p43). Continue west along Front, past the CBC (see p61), noting the Glenn Gould sculpture, honoring the eccentric pianist. You'll soon come to the **Rogers Centre** (see p67), and *The Audience*, Michael Snow's larger-than-life fans (see p43). Turn left on Spadina Avenue; crossing the bridge, look left to see Eldon Garnet's memorial commemorating Chinese laborers who helped build Canada's railroads. Continue south down Spadina turning right onto Fort York Boulevard, where you'll find Canoe Landing Park. Head back to Spadina from where it's only 5 minutes to the lake and, just west on Queens Quay, the lovely **Toronto Music Garden** (see p67).

See map on pp66–7

The Best of the Rest

Delightful and amusing exhibits displayed at Design Exchange

1 Design Exchange
MAP K4 ▪ 234 Bay St ▪ Open 10am–5pm Mon–Fri, noon–5pm Sat & Sun ▪ Adm to special exhibits

This gallery showcases innovative Canadian postwar design.

2 Toronto Railway Museum
MAP J5 ▪ 255 Bremner Blvd ▪ Open noon–5pm Wed–Sun ▪ Adm

Rolling stock and diesel and steam engines stand proud on the turntable of the John Street Roundhouse. Enjoy miniature train rides in summer.

3 401 Richmond Street
MAP H4 ▪ 401 Richmond St W

Many of the city's best artist-run galleries are based in this gorgeous old warehouse. Find great gifts and reading material at Swipe Design | Books + Objects.

4 Toronto Dominion Gallery of Inuit Art
MAP K4 ▪ 79 Wellington St W ▪ Open 8am–6pm Mon–Fri, 10am–4pm Sat & Sun

An outstanding collection of postwar Inuit sculpture (see p41).

5 Steam Whistle Brewing
MAP J5 ▪ 255 Bremner Blvd ▪ Open noon–6pm Mon–Thu, 11am–6pm Fri–Sun

This railroad roundhouse now functions as a microbrewery. Tour the facilities, then sample the beer.

6 Power Plant Contemporary Art Gallery
MAP K6 ▪ 231 Queens Quay W ▪ Open 10am–5pm Tue–Sun (until 8pm Thu); holiday Mondays

Toronto's premier contemporary art public gallery (see p40).

7 Fairmont Royal York
MAP K5 ▪ 100 Front St W

This grand château-style hotel (see p116), once the largest in the British Commonwealth, was built in 1928 by the Canadian Pacific Railway.

8 Air Canada Centre
MAP K5 ▪ 40 Bay St

Home to basketball's Raptors and hockey's Maple Leafs, the arena is in the old Toronto Postal Delivery Building. Carvings on the facade show the history of communications.

9 Exhibition Place
MAP A5

Princes' Gates herald the entrance to the Canadian National Exhibition's fairgrounds, hosting events such as the Royal Agricultural Winter Fair.

10 Commerce Court North
MAP L4 ▪ 25 King St W

The star among Toronto's early skyscrapers, this massive 34-story Romanesque structure housing the Canadian Imperial Bank of Commerce was the tallest building in Canada when completed in 1931.

Theaters

 1 Theatre Passe Muraille
MAP G3 ■ 16 Ryerson Ave
■ 416 504 7529

This venue has led the way with innovative Canadian productions since the 1960s, when it launched works developed by actors (see p51).

2 Princess of Wales Theatre
MAP J4 ■ 300 King St W ■ 416 872 1212

This venue for hit musicals opened in 1993, and was the first privately developed large theater the city had seen since 1907. The interior, by Toronto firm Yabu Pushelberg, spares no expense. Wall and ceiling murals are by American minimalist Frank Stella.

3 Fleck Dance Theatre
MAP K6 ■ 207 Queens Quay W ■ 416 973 4000

The crème de la crème of modern dance, by both local and visiting companies, has graced this stage.

4 Elgin Theatre
MAP L3 ■ 189 Yonge St ■ 1 855 622 2787 (tickets), 416 314 2871 (tours)

The lower half of the double-decker Elgin and Winter Garden Theatre Centre was built in 1913 as a movie house and features lavish gilding and a proscenium arch (see p50).

5 Ed Mirvish Theatre
MAP L3 ■ 244 Victoria St ■ 416 872 1212

Musicals have replaced vaudeville on the bill. The 1920s interior is a fantasy of gilt-framed mirrors, chandeliers, an epic staircase, and dome.

6 Winter Garden Theatre
MAP L3 ■ 189 Yonge St ■ 1 855 622 2787 (tickets), 416 314 2871 (tours)

This room high above Elgin Theatre is aptly named. On the ceiling, some 5,000 beech leaves glitter in the lantern light (see p50).

7 Royal Alexandra Theatre
MAP J4 ■ 260 King St W ■ 416 872 1212

Saved from demolition, this theater has been returned to Edwardian finery and features a dramatic mural.

The Royal Alexandra's stunning stage

8 Factory Theatre
MAP G4 ■ 125 Bathurst St ■ 416 504 9971

One of Toronto's oldest houses shows works by Canadian playwrights.

9 Bluma Appel Theatre
Devoted fans of Canada Stage's contemporary drama fill the seats in this theater (see p51).

10 Young People's Theatre
MAP M4 ■ 165 Front St E ■ 416 862 2222 www.youngpeoplestheatre.ca

This award-winning theater produces innovative plays for young viewers (see p48).

Ed Mirvish Theatre

See map on pp66–7

Bars and Clubs

1 Bar at Canoe
MAP K4 ▪ 66 Wellington St W
▪ 416 364 0054 ▪ Closed Sat & Sun

It's a heady experience sipping the perfect martini while gazing at the city from the top of a skyscraper. Bar at Canoe is the place to come for after-work power drinks *(see p57)*.

2 The Fifth Social Club
MAP J4 ▪ 225 Richmond St W (enter via alley) ▪ 416 979 3000 ▪ Open Thu–Sat ▪ Adm

Popular nightclub across two floors with original live shows and monthly theme parties. Head here for R&B and top 40 hits *(see p56)*.

3 Brassaii
MAP H4 ▪ 461 King St W ▪ 416 598 4730

A sophisticated place for a big night out. Expect great food followed by dancing Wed–Sat evening *(see p73)*.

4 Bar Hop
MAP H4 ▪ 391 King St W ▪ 647 352 7476

This place takes craft beer seriously. Choose from the 36 taps or from the seven-page beer menu.

5 The Chase
MAP L4 ▪ 10 Temperance St ▪ 647 346 7000

Take the elevator to the fifth floor of this heritage building and be dazzled by the polished, unpretentious service and sophisticated surroundings.

6 Cactus Club
MAP K4 ▪ First Canadian Place, 77 Adelaide St W ▪ 647 748 2025

Drinks at the Cactus Club include innovative creations such as a decadent take on a martini. The contemporary art on display is impressive.

7 Irish Embassy Pub & Grill
Map L5 ▪ 49 Yonge St ▪ 416 866 8282

Savor a drink at the mahogany bar or delicious pub food at one of the comfortable banquettes *(see p57)*.

8 Wheat Sheaf Tavern
MAP G4 ▪ 667 King St W ▪ 416 504 9912

Toronto's oldest tavern dates back to 1849. Enjoy chicken wings and a pint with TV sports, or go out on the deck.

9 Maison Mercer
MAP J4 ▪ 15 Mercer St ▪ 416 341 7777

This club pulls in some big name DJs. The brilliant roof terrace is open in summer.

10 Library Bar
MAP K5 ▪ 100 Front St W ▪ 416 860 5004

Tucked inside the Fairmont Royal York hotel *(see p70)*, this bar has a gentleman's-club atmosphere, with its book-lined walls and leather chairs. The cocktails are great.

The sophisticated bar at The Chase

Restaurants

1 Canoe
MAP K4 ■ 66 Wellington St W ■ 416 364 0054 ■ Closed Sat & Sun ■ $$$
Upscale Canadian dishes are the order of the day from chef John Horne. The views from the 54th-floor room are stunning *(see p55)*.

Marben's industrial-style interior

2 Marben
MAP H4 ■ 488 Wellington St W ■ 416 979 1990 ■ $$
With a fine selection of vegetarian and meat dishes, Marben's serves up delicious, creative cuisine.

3 Rodney's Oyster House
MAP H4 ■ 469 King St W ■ 416 363 8105 ■ $$
Two dozen types of oysters and grilled fish entice fans.

4 Luckee
MAP J4 ■ 328 Wellington St W ■ 416 935 0400 ■ $$
Toronto's own superstar chef Susur Lee applies his artistry to the ultimate small-plate meal – dim sum.

5 Le Sélect Bistro
MAP H4 ■ 432 Wellington St West ■ 416 596 6405 ■ $$
A much-loved French restaurant with classy curved booths. Good wine list.

PRICE CATEGORIES
Price categories include a three-course meal for one, half a bottle of wine, and all unavoidable extra charges including tax.
....
$ under $50 $$ $50–120 $$$ over $120

6 Bymark
MAP K4 ■ 66 Wellington St W ■ 416 777 1144 ■ $$
Some of the freshest fish in town and extravagant *foie gras* attract a well-heeled crowd. Top selection of boutique Californian wines.

7 Jacob's & Co
MAP H4 ■ 12 Brant St ■ 416 366 0200 ■ $$$
Dry-aged steaks are cooked to perfection at this modern take on the classic steak house.

8 Buca
MAP G4 ■ 604 King St W ■ 416 865 1600 ■ $$
Italian fare with a contemporary twist served by friendly staff.

9 Mercatto
MAP K4 ■ 330 Bay St ■ 416 306 0467 ■ Closed Sun, & Sat lunch ■ $$
Find home-cooked food and excellent wines at this down-to-earth eatery. Popular with locals on weekdays.

Seafood dish, Mercatto

10 Brassaii
MAP H4 ■ 461 King St W ■ 416 598 4730 ■ $$
This modern restaurant in an old warehouse features a romantic courtyard. Chef Marcus Monteiro's delicious Mediterranean cuisine draws a trendy crowd.

See map on pp66–7

🔟 Downtown

Toronto is a city of neighborhoods, each with a distinct identity and many with an ethnic flavor, making it one of the most multicultural North American cities. In Chinatown, vendors compete with shoppers for sidewalk space, and restaurants offer everything from take-out buns to sit-down banquets. The multicultural mix has its fullest expression in Kensington Market, where Jamaican patty shops rub shoulders with Portuguese fish shops. Farther west is Little Italy, centered on College Street, while the downtown core has the upscale shopping area of Yorkville and many fine cultural institutions.

Wood carving at the AGO

DOWNTOWN

① **Top 10 Sights**
see pp75–7

① **Restaurants and Cafés**
see p83

① **The Best of the Rest**
see p78

① **Bars and Pubs**
see p81

① **West Queen West Shops**
see p80

① **Bloor St and Yorkville Shops**
see p79

① **Ethnic Eats**
see p82

1 CF Toronto Eaton Centre

While it might seem strange that a shopping center is one of the most popular tourist attractions in the city – according to the numbers, at any rate – this retail complex is simply a very popular place to shop, meet, hang out, and people-watch, with crowds of boisterous teenagers attesting to this fact. Its massive size, with more than 300 stores, ensures that visitors can find practically anything they would want to buy here. Numerous restaurants, fast-food counters, and specialty treat shops round out the choices (see pp30–31).

2 Art Gallery of Ontario

Particularly strong in historical and contemporary Canadian works, as well as host to important exhibitions, the AGO one of the country's top art galleries (see pp20–21).

Royal Ontario Museum Crystal facade

3 Royal Ontario Museum

Canada's premier museum has more than six million artifacts showcasing art, archeology, science, and nature (see pp12–13).

4 Kensington Market
MAP H2

This funky neighborhood, in a small pocket west of Spadina, is the heart of multicultural Toronto – a place where vendors from across the globe have set up shop. An array of fruits, vegetables, and bulk dry goods spill out into the narrow sidewalks, while music blasts from open doors and loudspeakers. Pedestrians jostle with cyclists, and traffic moves at a snail's pace, especially on Saturdays. Leave the car behind and wander through the streets, soaking up the atmosphere. Try a Jamaican patty on Baldwin Street or browse vintage clothes at Exile (62 Kensington Ave) and contemporary fashion at Fresh Collective (274 Augusta Ave).

Casa Loma, resembling a medieval castle, looming high above downtown

5 Casa Loma

This grand castle-style mansion is a monument to the tastes and vision of Sir Henry Pellatt, a prominent financier, who, in 1911, commissioned renowned architect E. J. Lennox to build him a home. This immense architectural under-taking was on a scale never before seen in a private Canadian residence, with 98 rooms, 12 baths, 5,000 electric lights, and an elevator. Its $3.5 million cost helped bankrupt Sir Henry after he and his wife moved in, but its opulence remains in the extravagant rooms and fine fur-nishings (see pp24–5).

Elton's platforms, Bata Shoe Museum

6 Bata Shoe Museum

MAP C3 ▪ 327 Bloor St W ▪ Open 10am–5pm Mon–Sat, noon–5pm Sun ▪ Adm

This specialized museum, founded by Sonia Bata, celebrates footwear form and function over the ages and around the world. Echoing a stylized shoebox, the building houses four galleries exhibiting everything from Roman sandals to Elton John's platforms. The exhibit of Chinese bound-foot shoes is definitely not for the squeamish. The museum regularly holds interesting footwear-themed exhibitions (see p40).

NATURAL AIR CONDITIONING

During the hot and humid days of a Toronto summer, Lake Ontario water does double duty. An innovative project utilizes the cold temperature of deep lake water – from intake pipes 270 ft (82 m) deep – to provide chilled energy for air conditioning Toronto's downtown high-rises and large facilities such as the Air Canada Centre (see p70). After the transfer of energy, the water is returned not to the lake but to the city's water-supply system, where it serves another crucial cooling function – as drinking water.

7 Yorkville

MAP C3–D3

In the 1960s, this neighborhood was ground zero for hippies and youth culture; today, it is ground zero for establishment culture and the city's most upscale shopping. Shops on Cumberland Street and Yorkville Avenue, between Bay Street and Avenue Road, sell luxury cosmetics, jewelry, designer fashions, antiques, and leather luggage. Restaurants and bars cater to equally refined palates and wallets, and there are many fine-art galleries, exhibiting some of Canada's top names.

⑧ Campbell House
MAP K3 ▪ 160 Queen St W ▪
416 597 0227 ▪ Open 9:30am–4:30pm
Tue–Fri, noon–4:30pm Sat & Sun
(Sundays only Jun–Aug); closed Jan,
Good Fri–Easter Mon, Thanksgiving
weekend, Dec 25–31 ▪ Adm

The city's oldest remaining building,
this Georgian mansion was built in
1822 for William Campbell, an Upper
Canada judge. In 1972, the building
was moved from its original location
on Adelaide Street to its present
spot, restored, and opened to the
public. Guided tours are available.

⑨ City Hall
MAP K3 ▪ 100 Queen St

When City Hall opened in 1965, the
result of an international design
competition won by Finnish architect
Viljo Revell, the building was highly
controversial – the two curving
towers caused an uproar. It has since
become a prized landmark of the
city, and the central plaza, Nathan
Phillips Square, a lively symbol
of civic life – a place for political
demonstrations, winter ice skating, a
summer farmers' market, concerts,
and celebrations. Inside are murals
and fabulous artworks (see p43).

⑩ Chinatown
MAP H2–H3

A steady flow of Chinese immigrants
keeps Toronto's Chinatown one of
the most vibrant in North America.
Hundreds of restaurants cater to all
tastes and budgets alongside shops
selling Oriental wares (see p59).

Busy street in Chinatown

A DOWNTOWN WALK

Gardiner Museum of Ceramic Art
Philosopher's Walk
University of Toronto
Royal Ontario Museum
University of Toronto Art Centre
Hart House
Convocation Hall
Chinatown
Lee Garden

▶ MORNING

Start the day at the **Gardiner
Museum of Ceramic Art** (see p78),
taking 90 minutes to peruse the
permanent collections and visiting exhibits. On your way out,
pop into the gift shop to have
a look at the unique crafts.

Head north to Bloor Street and
turn left, walking a half block to
the iron gates of Philosophers'
Walk, beside the **Royal Ontario
Museum** (see pp12–15). Take this
charming footpath, which follows
the course of the now-buried
Taddle Creek, exiting at Hoskin
Street in the heart of the **University
of Toronto** campus (see p78).
Wander south to the Late Gothic
Revival Hart House, lunching at
Gallery Grill (7 Hart House Circle).

AFTERNOON

After lunch, poke around the
stately common rooms and
library of Hart House, noting the
paintings throughout. Check out
the Canadian art on display at
Justina M. Barnicke Gallery, too.

From Hart House turn right
toward University College and
some of the most historic
buildings on campus. Stop by
the Laidlaw Wing to visit the
University of Toronto Art Centre
(see p41). Just to the south, on
King's College Circle, is the 1906
Convocation Hall, with its Ionic-
column-supported dome. Peek
inside if the doors are unlocked.

From here, head to a feast at **Lee
Garden** (see p82) on Spadina
Avenue in **Chinatown**, a couple
of blocks' stroll south and west.

See map on pp74–5

The Best of the Rest

 1 **Gardiner Museum of Ceramic Art**
MAP C3 ▪ 111 Queen's Park ▪ 416 586 8080 ▪ Open 10am–6pm Mon–Thu, 10am–9pm Fri, 10am–5pm Sat & Sun ▪ Adm

Historic and modern pieces from around the world (see p40).

2 **Bloor Street**
MAP C3–D3

This street is an upscale shopping strip of high-end fashion and home-decor stores (see p58).

3 **University of Toronto**
MAP H1–J1

A sprawling campus of green spaces and historic stone buildings dominates a huge swath of the central city, fanning out north, east, and west from Queen's Park (see p42).

4 **Old City Hall**
MAP K3 ▪ 60 Queen St W

The entranceway columns carry carved caricatures of local politicians, with one exception – a straight-faced depiction of the architect. The edifice is now a courthouse (see p43).

5 **Osgoode Hall**
MAP K3 ▪ 130 Queen St W ▪ 416 947 3300 ▪ Open Aug–late Jun: 11:45am–2pm Mon–Fri

Ontario's first law school now houses upper provincial courts. The interior of the building is magnificent.

6 **Spadina Museum**
MAP C2 ▪ 285 Spadina Rd ▪ Open Jan–mid-Apr: noon–5pm Sat & Sun; mid-Apr–Aug: noon–5pm Tue–Sun; Sep–Dec: noon–4pm Tue–Fri (to 5pm Sat & Sun) ▪ Adm

A restored 1866 house with exhibits from the 1920s to the 1940s. Tours only.

A preserved room, Spadina Museum

7 **West Queen West**
MAP A4–B4

A neighborhood of eclectic shops, galleries, and cafés (see p80).

8 **The Annex**
MAP C2–C3

This area of upscale, leafy sidestreets and lively restaurants, pubs, and shops north of Bloor Street makes for a great stroll.

9 **Little Italy**
MAP B3–B4

Shops and delis bustle all day long; bars and restaurants buzz at night.

10 **Ontario Legislative Building**
MAP K1 ▪ 1 Queen's Park ▪ Open mid-May–Aug: 8:30am–5:30pm daily; Sep–mid-May: 8:30am–4:30pm Mon–Fri

This stately building is set in a park dotted with statues and cannons. Watch politicians in action from the gallery or join in a tour (see p60).

Trees in blossom in front of Osgoode Hall

Bloor Street and Yorkville Shops

1 TNT (The New Trend)
MAP D3 ■ 87 Avenue Rd

Yorkville Village's trendiest tenants attract the stylish set with their designer clothes. An adjacent, 6,000 sq ft extension store, TNT Concept, opened in fall 2017.

2 Holt Renfrew
MAP D3 ■ 50 Bloor St W

This world-class department store features high fashion, as well as more affordable clothing from its own label, top perfumes and cosmetics, a hair salon, epicure store, café, and free personal shopping service.

3 George C
MAP C2 ■ 21 Hazleton Ave

This store occupies a converted Victorian residence and stocks exclusive and adventurous high fashion for men and women. The selectively curated and reverently displayed pieces include exquisitely crafted boots by Rocco P and leather fashions by Drome.

4 Harry Rosen
MAP C3 ■ 82 Bloor St W

Head-to-toe service is writ large at this menswear store featuring apparel from top design houses, including Canali and Hugo Boss. They stock suits, trousers, shirts, shoes, and accessories.

5 David's
MAP D3
■ 66 Bloor St W

Shoe lovers will go wild among the stylish footwear from hot designers here.

6 Pusateri's
MAP D3 ■ 57 Yorkville Ave

Food aficionados will love the luxury grocery items such as caviar and truffle oil, and flavorsome prepared foods.

Fashion goods displayed at Roots

Delicious shortbread basket from Pusateri's

7 Roots
MAP C3 ■ 80 Bloor St W

Quality sportswear, casual clothes, and leather goods for every member of the family are on offer from this Canadian brand.

8 L'Atelier Grigorian
MAP D3 ■ 70 Yorkville Ave

The city's premier location for jazz, classical, and world music, L'Atelier Grigorian has been a regular stop for audiophiles passing through the city since 1980.

9 Liss Gallery
MAP C3 ■ 112 Cumberland St

Cutting-edge exhibitions of contemporary paintings, photography, and sculptures are held here, often with the artist in attendance.

10 Thomas Hinds Tobacconists
MAP D3 ■ 8 Cumberland St

This smoker's paradise includes a walk-in humidor with a full range of Cuban and Latin American cigars, and two lounges in which to enjoy them. Stellar selection of tobaccos, cigarettes, and accessories.

See map on pp74–5

West Queen West Shops

1 **C Squared**
MAP G4 ▪ 693 Queen St W
(just west of Bathurst)

The impressive selection of Campers, Marc, and hand-crafted Cydwoqs attracts those looking for funky footwear.

2 **Morba**
MAP G4 ▪ 665 Queen St W (just west of Bathurst)

Mid-century modern emporium with loads of second-hand teak, light fixtures, and Finnish glass, plus 1950s-inspired bits-and-bobs for the kitchen and office.

Second-hand typewriter, Morba

3 **Anthropologie**
MAP B4 ▪ 761 Queen St W

This store's setting – in a wonderful converted former church with stained-glass windows – is as beautiful as the clothes, shoes, accessories, and home furnishings it sells.

4 **Heel Boy**
MAP B4 ▪ 773 Queen St W

This is a hip shoe boutique for men and women. Prices ($100 to $400-plus) are good, and the quality and selection are excellent. They stock everything – from sandals to espadrilles to lace-up booties.

5 **Drake General Store**
MAP A4 ▪ 1144 Queen St W
(at Beaconsfield Ave)

Attached to The Drake's Hotel, this Canadiana shop is a great place to shop for gifts. There are branches at Yonge and Eglinton and in the Bay at Yonge and Queen.

6 **Type Books**
MAP B4 ▪ 883 Queen St W
(across from Trinity Bellwoods Park)

A cozy independent with a great range of fiction and design titles and an inspired children's section.

7 **The Paper Place**
MAP B4 ▪ 887 Queen St W

This Japanese-inspired store stocks a gorgeous selection of Chiyogami silk-screened paper, as well as ribbon, cards, and wrapping paper.

8 **Fred Perry**
MAP A4 ▪ 964 Queen St W

Mod-style threads from this UK designer chain include Laurel-insignia collared tees, trainers, and classic leather sports bags.

9 **Lavish & Squalor**
MAP J4 ▪ 253 Queen St W

Known for soy wax candles in amber jars, this hip shop and café stocks various Canadian treasures, from raw denim apparel to home accessories.

10 **Coal Miner's Daughter**
MAP B4 ▪ 744 Queen St W
(at Niagara St)

There are pretty, alternative designs and a handmade ethos at this independent boutique. They sell local and Swedish jewelry and vintage shoes.

Fashions at Coal Miner's Daughter

Bars and Pubs

The Oxley, a stylish gastro pub

1 **The Oxley**
MAP C3 ■ 121 Yorkville Ave
■ 647 348 1300

In a neighborhood packed with wine bars, the Oxley is a comfortable gastro pub offering down-to-earth grub and a great range of beers.

2 **The Queen and Beaver**
MAP L2 ■ 35 Elm St ■ 647 347 2712

This quirky take on an English pub puts an equally tasty twist on its fare – try the unusual stilton ice cream.

3 **Dog and Bear**
MAP A4 ■ 1100 Queen St W
■ 647 352 8601

A friendly pub hung with Union Jacks and sporting dark red flocked wallpaper. Sports-mad with numerous screens, and DJs on weekends.

4 **The Roof Lounge**
MAP C2 ■ 4 Avenue Rd ■ 416 924 5471

Snag a seat on the 18th-floor terrace for the view, or savor the warm atmosphere inside *(see p57)*.

5 **Lula Lounge**
MAP A4 ■ 1585 Dundas St W
■ 416 588 0307 ■ Adm

Salsa gets the hips swaying, as rum cocktails loosen you up at this Little Portugal hotspot *(see p56)*.

6 **Cameron House**
MAP H3 ■ 408 Queen St W
■ 416 703 0811 ■ Adm (for backroom shows)

Hang out with the locals and catch great local roots, folk, and indie bands in this ornate yet casual bar. The changing murals on the facade are a local landmark *(see p57)*.

7 **180 Panorama**
MAP D3 ■ 55 Bloor St W
■ 416 967 0000 ■ Adm

Not for acrophobics, this bar's patios, on the 51st floor of the Manulife Centre, are the city's highest.

8 **d|bar**
MAP D3 ■ 60 Yorkville Ave
■ 416 963 6010

Linger over a cocktail or glass of chardonnay in this chic bar, then do some people-watching *(see p56)*.

Cozy interior of The Drake Lounge

9 **The Drake Lounge**
MAP A4 ■ 1150 Queen St W
■ 416 531 5042

Recline on a comfy sofa beside the fireplace while taking in the scene, including the Raw Bar peddling its oysters. Afterwards, check out the live music or art happening downstairs in the underground bar.

10 **The Paddock**
MAP G4 ■ 178 Bathurst St
■ 416 504 9997

Although red leather banquettes prompt a twinge of 1950s nostalgia, this bar is rooted in the 21st century.

See map on pp74–5

Ethnic Eats

1 Bahn Mi Boys
MAP L2 ■ 399 Yonge St
■ 416 977 0303 ■ $

Traditional Vietnamese *bahn mi* baguettes (stuffed with grilled pork, sausage or paté, grated veg and cilantro) are served with pulled pork or squid. Try the kimchi fries.

2 Boulevard Café
MAP C3 ■ 161 Harbord St
■ 416 961 7676 ■ $

The city's oldest Peruvian restaurant offers grilled meats and seafood. Tapas are served in the upstairs lounge and on the patio in summer.

3 Lee Garden
MAP H2 ■ 331 Spadina Ave
■ 416 593 9524 ■ Closed lunch ■ $$

This Cantonese restaurant is the place to go for tasty chow mein, barbecued pork, and fresh seafood.

4 Banjara Indian Cuisine
MAP B3 ■ 796 Bloor St W
■ 416 963 9360 ■ $$

An unfussy, diner-like interior belies the fine Indian cooking for which Banjara has become famous.

An authentic setting at Julie's Cuban

5 Julie's Cuban
MAP A4 ■ 202 Dovercourt Rd
■ 416 532 7397 ■ $$

Checkered table cloths, vintage salt and pepper shakers, a warm welcome, and good, earthy Cuban food.

Italian fare, Café Diplomatico

6 Café Diplomatico
MAP B3 ■ 594 College St
■ 416 534 4637 ■ $

The patio is the place to be at this Little Italy institution. Pizza, pasta, and panzerotti are on the menu, but it's also popular for people-watching.

7 Korea House
MAP B3 ■ 666 Bloor St W
■ 416 536 8666 ■ $

This family-run restaurant cooks up traditional Korean fare. Try the Korean rice wines or *soju*, distilled liquors flavored with fruit or flowers.

8 El Trompo
MAP H2 ■ 277 Augusta Ave
■ 416 260 0097 ■ $

A fun, lively Mexican place right in the heart of Kensington Market. If you're lucky you'll snag a seat on the patio to take in the streetlife.

9 Sashimi Island
MAP B3 ■ 635 College St
■ 416 535 1888 ■ $

One of many all-you-can-eat sushi joints. Refined Japanese dining it is not, but if you are just after *maki* rolls, then this will hit the spot.

10 Churrasqueira do Sardinha
MAP B3 ■ 707 College St ■ 416 531 1120 ■ $

Portuguese rotisserie chicken is a local tradition. This spotless takeout and eat-in spot is a favorite, known for its spicy sauce ribs.

See map on pp74–5

Restaurants and Cafés

 Aunties and Uncles
MAP B3 ▪ 74 Lippincott S
▪ 416 324 1375 ▪ $

A quirky, retro-style diner that offers comfort food favorites such as Canadian cheddar grilled cheese and cinnamon french toast.

 Fresh
MAP C4 ▪ 326 Bloor St W
▪ 416 599 4442 ▪ $

A vegetarian eatery providing a filling meal and loads of choice. Noodle bowls and vitamin-packed juices suit all who need a healthy pick-up. Branches at Queen W and Crawford, and Richmond and Spadina.

 Noce
MAP B4 ▪ 875 Queen St W
▪ 416 504 3463 ▪ $$

Noce serves house-made pasta, pizzas, meat, and seafood, and all of its dishes incorporate a creative, wood-fired element.

④ **ALO**
MAP H4 ▪ 163 Spadina Ave
▪ 416 260 2222 ▪ $$$

ALO serves a nine-course French tasting menu, called one of Toronto's "most remarkable" dining experiences, in a sedate room of a Victorian building. For a mid-priced meal, sit at the bar.

⑤ **Buca Yorkville**
MAP C3 ▪ 53 Scollard St
▪ 416 962 2822 ▪ $$$

A seafood-oriented Italian restaurant known not just for the freshness and variety of its fish dishes but also for the creative pastas and pizzas.

Stylish interiors of Buca Yorkville

PRICE CATEGORIES

Price categories include a three-course meal for one, half a bottle of wine, and all unavoidable extra charges including tax.

$ under $50 $$ $50–120 $$$ over $120

⑥ **La Palette**
MAP H2 ▪ 492 Queen St W
▪ 416 929 4900 ▪ $$

This bohemian space tempts with good-value French food, and takes its pedigree to heart, offering horse tenderloin to adventurous diners.

⑦ **Opus**
MAP C3 ▪ 37 Prince Arthur Ave
▪ 416 921 3105 ▪ $$

This refined dining room has one of the best wine lists in the city. Tuna tartare with caviar, and the roasted meats get top marks.

⑧ **Mildred's Temple Kitchen**
MAP A5 ▪ 85 Hanna Ave
▪ 416 588 5695 ▪ $

Pioneers of the brunch trend, Mildred's is still going strong 20 years later. Expect classic dishes featuring seasonal, regional ingredients.

⑨ **Dark Horse Espresso Bar**
MAP H3 ▪ 215 Spadina Ave
▪ 416 979 1200 ▪ $

Its personal feel and great-quality coffee make the Dark Horse the ideal spot for a pick-me-up.

⑩ **Lai Wah Heen**
MAP K3 ▪ 108 Chestnut St
▪ 416 977 9899 ▪ $$

Translating to "luxurious meeting place," this elegant eatery has been serving first-rate dim sum since 1995.

TOP 10 East

This region of contrasts has some of the city's grandest old mansions on the stately Jarvis and Sherbourne streets. Cabbagetown, originally a working-class Irish immigrant neighborhood with Victorian cottages and rowhouses, has now been transformed into an upscale district of urban professionals. The area has many historic sights as well as a vibrant streetlife thanks to the lively gay village along Church Street, the Greek and Macedonian enclave of the Danforth, and the fresh-food destination of St. Lawrence Market. To the south, a complex of Victorian buildings has been converted into the Distillery Historic District, a popular shopping and entertainment destination.

Mackenzie House exhibit

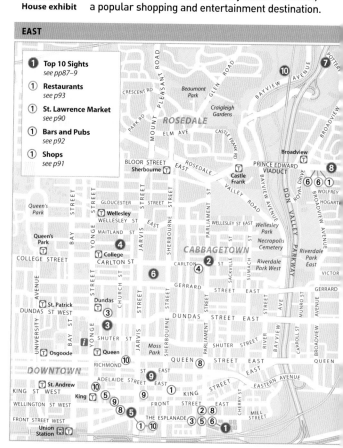

EAST

- **1** Top 10 Sights *see pp87–9*
- **1** Restaurants *see p93*
- **1** St. Lawrence Market *see p90*
- **1** Bars and Pubs *see p92*
- **1** Shops *see p91*

Previous pages Tranquil spot in Georgian Bay Islands National Park

Distillery Historic District

1 Distillery Historic District

This Victorian industrial district is now one of the city's most interesting and picturesque. Pedestrian-only cobblestone streets lead past old warehouses and historic factories stunningly preserved and renovated to house galleries, restaurants, performance venues, and specialty shops (see pp26–7).

2 Cabbagetown
MAP E3–E4

One of Toronto's oldest subdivisions, dating to the 1840s, this district was a working-class community well into the 1970s. Many of the cottages and Victorian homes have since been renovated, and it is now an upscale residential enclave that makes for a pleasant stroll. On the east side is Riverdale Park and its delightful Riverdale Farm (see p49). Across the street, set within the grounds of the Necropolis Cemetery, is an 1872 chapel, a Gothic Revival treasure. At the north end of Cabbagetown, St. James Cemetery, Toronto's oldest, has many beautiful crypts.

Necropolis Cemetery, Cabbagetown

3 Mackenzie House
MAP L3 ■ 82 Bond St ■ 416 392 6915 ■ Open Jan–Apr: noon–5pm Sat & Sun; May–early Sep: noon–5pm Tue–Sun; Sep–Dec: noon–4pm Tue–Fri, noon–5pm Sat & Sun ■ Adm

This Greek Revival rowhouse, built in 1858, was the home of Toronto's first mayor, William Lyon Mackenzie. Now a period museum, it features a re-created print shop and a gallery with changing exhibitions.

A colorful building representative of the vibrant Church Street scene

④ Church Street
MAP L1–L2

The hub of Toronto's Gay and Lesbian Village, Church Street from Carleton Street to north of Wellesley Street, is vibrant day and night. Restaurants and bars cater to an out crowd, and specialty shops abound. Pick up a copy of the free daily newspaper *Xtra!* for listings of everything the village has to offer.

⑤ St. Lawrence Market
MAP M5 ▪ 92–95 Front St E

Considered one of the world's great markets, the St. Lawrence complex consists of South Market and North Market (currently being redeveloped). The 120-plus vendors sell great fresh food products, and there is also an antiques market *(see p90)*.

DON RIVER

The Don is one of the defining natural features of Toronto. Flowing east of downtown into Lake Ontario, the steep river valley cuts a swath through the city. While industrial use of the river has degraded the water, naturalization projects have started the long process of restoring the valley to ecological health. The ribbon of linked green spaces following the Don's course means that you can hike and cycle right through the center of the city.

⑥ Allan Gardens
MAP M2

This large park embodies the contradictions of the downtown eastside: it is both grand and gritty. Best explored during the day, the gardens, which first opened in 1860, contain a delightful glass-and-metal conservatory complex consisting of six greenhouses built in 1910, each with a different climate zone. Inside, the exuberant displays of seasonal and permanent greenery and flowers delight the senses.

⑦ Todmorden Mills Heritage Site
MAP F2 ▪ 67 Pottery Rd ▪ Historic Buildings: Open Jan–May & Sep–Dec: noon–4pm Wed–Fri (to 4:30pm Sat & Sun); Jun–Aug: 10am–4:30pm Tue–Fri (to 7:30pm Thu), noon–5pm Sat & Sun ▪ Adm ▪ Grounds: Open daily

This collection of late 18th-century buildings imparts the feel of a historic village, and fine examples of the original industrial architecture pepper the site. Two of the houses – the 1797 Terry Cottage and 1800s Helliwell House – have been restored with period furnishings. The Paper Mill Gallery and Theatre stages performances and art shows. A wild flower preserve bursts with trilliums in spring, and trails offer lots of wildlife-spotting opportunities.

8 The Danforth
MAP F3

Linked to downtown by the 1918 Prince Edward Viaduct, which spans the Don River Valley, the Danforth has been home to thriving Greek and Macedonian communities since the 1950s. In early August, the weeklong Taste of the Danforth street festival is a smorgasbord of tasty treats and entertainment.

9 Toronto's First Post Office
MAP M4 ■ 260 Adelaide St E ■ 416 865 1833 ■ Open 9am–5:30pm Mon–Fri, 10am–4pm Sat, noon–4pm Sun ■ Adm by donation

This working post office and museum opened in 1833 and is the only surviving example of a British-era post office in Canada. Here, you can write a letter with a quill pen and have it stamped with a distinctive cancellation mark: "York-Toronto 1833." There is also a topographic model of 1830s Toronto, period furniture, and 19th-century repro-duction ink wells and sealing wax.

Toronto's First Post Office

10 Evergreen Brick Works
MAP E2 ■ 550 Bayview Ave

The smokestack is just one of the historic features that remain at this once-thriving industrial complex, which opened in 1889 to produce bricks using clay found on site. The quarry has been returned to nature as a park with ponds and meadows, and the industrial buildings redevel-oped as a sustainable development showcase. There is also a restaurant and adventure playground (see p45).

A CABBAGETOWN STROLL

Wellesley Street • Wellesley Cottages • Wellesley Park • Salisbury Ave • Sumach Street • Metcalfe St • Necropolis Cemetery • Jet Fuel • Winchester Café • Riverdale Farm • Peartree Restaurant • Sackville St • Riverdale Park

▶ MORNING

Begin your day at Jet Fuel (519 Parliament Street) with a strong espresso. After your caffeine jolt, turn right and walk north to Wellesley Street, then turn right again and walk east to take in the charming Victorian architecture. Note the strange animal and face carvings on No. 314. Explore the lanes running north, including Wellesley Cottages, a courtyard with seven gabled cottages tucked behind the street. As you come to the end of Wellesley, spend a few moments wandering through Wellesley Park, enjoying the view across the Don Valley.

Backtrack to Wellesley and turn left onto Sumach Street; its charming houses are classic **Cabbagetown** (see p87). Note Second Empire-style No. 420–422, built in 1886, and the English cottage style of Nos 404–408. Turn left at Winchester Street; Necropolis Cemetery will be on the left. Peek into the chapel to admire the stained glass.

AFTERNOON

For lunch, head back along Winchester Street to Parliament Street, where you'll find Peartree Restaurant (No. 507). After lunch, meander through the compact streets – Metcalfe, Salisbury, and Sackville – before walking east to Riverdale Park and its **Riverdale Farm** (see p49). Cute Winchester Café (161 Winchester Street), dispensing refreshments through a side window, is situated just across the street from the park's northwest corner.

See map on pp86–7

St. Lawrence Market

Undercover market stalls selling fresh food items, St. Lawrence Market

1 South Market
Open 8am–6pm Tue–Thu, 8am–7pm Fri, 5am–5pm Sat
Opened in 1845 as Toronto's second City Hall, this building now houses a thriving public market – and some of the tastiest, freshest meats, cheese, produce, and breads around.

2 North Market
Open 5am–early afternoon Sat
North Market is being redeveloped (due to open in 2019). The fresh food vendors are currently operating from a block south at 125 Esplanade.

3 European Delight
This Ukrainian mainstay in South Market's lower level serves up home-made favorites – cabbage rolls, *perogies* (dumplings) – for takeout; you can also buy them frozen.

4 Sunday Antique Market
From 5am on Sunday, vendors offer piles of knick-knacks as well as more serious pieces such as military collectibles and mid-century design classics (at 125 Esplanade while the North Market is being refurbished).

5 Montreal Bagels
Locals love St. Urbain Bakery's dense, chewy buns (South Market). Their bagel-cooking method – which involves boiling then baking them in a wood-fired oven – hails from the French-Canadian city of Montreal.

6 Alex Farm Products
This cheese-lover's paradise, in South Market, sells every kind of cheese imaginable, from French cantal to the most pungent of blues. Good raw-milk cheese selection.

7 Buskers and Craft-Sellers
Lively street action is part of the charm of market Saturdays, as buskers entertain and craftspeople ply their wares outside the south buildings during warmer months.

8 Peameal Bacon Sandwiches
Quintessentially Canadian, and perfect to fuel up for the day, the kaiser buns at South Market's Carousel Bakery are stuffed with salty, peameal-encrusted pork.

9 Market Gallery
Open 10am–4pm Tue–Fri, 9am–4pm Sat ■ Adm for some exhibits
Artifacts and historical photographs of the city are exhibited in themed shows in the old council chamber on the second floor of South Market.

10 South Market – Lower Floor
Below the market's main floor are stalls with items such as accessories and hats, and jams and chutneys. There are also health-food stores, greengrocers, and a coffee shop.

Shops

1 Negash & Dessa
MAP F3 ▪ 161 Danforth Ave
▪ 416 462 9306

This shop sells an excellent range of accessories including a sophisticated range of leather goods, and sleek silver jewelry too.

2 The Big Carrot
MAP F3 ▪ Carrot Common Complex, 348 Danforth Ave ▪ 416 466 2129

Lovers of organic foods and natural body care will love this large and well-stocked grocery store, where they can recharge by sampling the delicious prepared foods and organic juices on offer here.

3 Soma Chocolate
MAP E5 ▪ 32 Tank House Lane
▪ 416 815 7662

This is one for the chocolate cognoscenti. Sample the divine confections or try a cup of steaming Mayan hot chocolate, redolent with spices.

Gadabout, located in Leslieville

4 Gadabout
MAP F4 ▪ 1300 Queen St E
▪ 416 463 1254

Get lost in time at this tiny vintage store. Oddments from around the globe are packed into display cases, and there are plenty of vintage finds.

5 Bergo Designs
MAP E5 ▪ 28 Tank House Lane
▪ 416 861 1821

This Distillery Historic District boutique calls itself a gallery of design. Cutting-edge items, from jewelry to furniture to kitchen gadgets, could double as artworks, making them perfect gifts.

6 John Fluevog
MAP E5 ▪ 4 Trinity St ▪ 416 583 1970

Bad-boy cobbler Fluevog, who hails from Vancouver and has been making his solid, unusual shoes for years, now sells his footwear in the vibrant Distillery Historic District's Boiler House Complex.

7 Artsmarket
MAP F4 ▪ 1114 Queen St E
▪ 416 546 8464

Artists, vintage collectors, and craftspeople display their vastly differing wares in small, close-knit spaces. Good fun on a lively Leslieville block.

8 Ethel
MAP E4 ▪ 327 Queen St E
▪ 416 778 6608

Elegant teak dining tables, glass and acrylic coffee tables, and other nifty pieces from the 1960s and 1970s, at reasonable prices.

9 Kristapsons
MAP F4 ▪ 1095 Queen St E
▪ 416 466 5152

Pacific salmon, cold-smoked on the premises using a secret recipe, is all you'll find in this store – but what a find. Those in the know claim it ranks among the world's best.

10 Henry's
MAP L4 ▪ 119 Church St
▪ 416 868 0872

Everything a photographer needs, from the latest digital cameras to vintage Leica lenses, and necessities such as film, batteries, photo paper, and a quality developing service.

See map on pp86–7

Bars and Pubs

1 **Betty's**
MAP M4 ■ 240 King St E
■ 416 368 1300

This pub offers beers on tap, tasty food such Montreal smoked meat on rye, billiard tables, and a patio.

2 **Mill Street Brew Pub**
MAP E5 ■ 21 Tank House Lane
■ 416 681 0338

Sample the 13 brews on tap while gazing on the vats of beer fermenting in the glass-walled brewery.

3 **Imperial Pub Tavern**
MAP L3 ■ 54 Dundas St E
■ 416 977 4667

Customers treasure the circular bar and jukeboxes playing old jazz hits in this no-frills place.

4 **Stout Irish Pub**
MAP E4 ■ 221 Carlton St
■ 647 344 7676

With a changing beer menu, creative pub food, and fun trivia nights, this tavern draws a devoted clientele.

5 **Consort Bar**
MAP L4 ■ 37 King St E
■ 416 863 3131

Relish the great whiskeys and masterfully mixed cocktails in this dignified bar at the Omni King Edward Hotel (see p116).

The stately Consort Bar

6 **Dora Keogh**
MAP F3 ■ 141 Danforth Ave
■ 416 778 1804

A reconstructed 1890s Irish pub, with dark-wood benches, stools, and little tables. Good selection of beers and whiskeys. Live music most nights.

Irish music session, Ceílí Cottage

7 **Ceílí Cottage**
MAP F4 ■ 1301 Queen St E
■ 416 406 1301

Snug, rustic Irish bar with excellent food and good hand-pulled beer (no bottles), and traditional Irish music on Tuesday nights.

8 **C'est What?**
MAP L5 ■ 67 Front St E
■ 416 867 9499

A casual spot with 35 microbrews on tap, some, such as the hemp, rye, and coffee brews, produced exclusively for the pub. Live music some nights and Sunday afternoons.

9 **Pravda Vodka House**
MAP L4 ■ 44 Wellington St E
■ 416 366 0303

Enjoy Russian-inspired food and endless vodka at this restaurant with Soviet-themed decor (see p56).

10 **BeerBistro**
MAP L4 ■ 18 King St E
■ 416 861 9872

Beer is taken seriously here with an enormous selection. Many menu items incorporate beers too.

Restaurants

PRICE CATEGORIES

Price categories include a three-course meal for one, half a bottle of wine, and all unavoidable extra charges including tax.

$ under $50 $$ $50–120 $$$ over $120

 Lady Marmalade
MAP F4 ▪ 898 Queen St E
▪ 647 351 7645 ▪ $

Serving eggs Benedict and Mexican dishes with organic, seasonal produce, this friendly, locals' spot offers all-day breakfast and lunch.

2 Pizza Libretto
MAP F3 ▪ 550 Danforth Ave
▪ 416 466 0400 ▪ $

This lively spot serves up the most authentic Neapolitan pizzas in town. Reserve ahead for a table or perch at the window.

 Mezes
MAP F3 ▪ 456 Danforth Ave ▪ 416 361 5634 ▪ $

This Greektown favorite encourages sharing – appropriate since Mezes means "small plates." Try the steamed mussels, spicy feta and *saganaki* – the cheese dish that arrives at the table flambéed.

4 Batifole
MAP F4 ▪ 744 Gerrard St E
▪ 416 462 9965 ▪ $$

Devoted Francophiles flock to this unpretentious restaurant on the outer edge of Chinatown East for classics such as *cassoulet* and *soupe de poissons*.

5 Sauvignon Bistro
MAP B2 ▪ 1862 Queen St E
▪ 416 686 1998 ▪ $$

This cozy spot is a haunt for locals of the Beach. Relax on the sidewalk patio and enjoy steak frites, duck confit or other bistro-style dishes.

6 Allen's
MAP F3 ▪ 143 Danforth Ave
▪ 416 463 3086 ▪ $$

Grab a wooden booth at the front of this pub-restaurant or eat out on one of the best patios in the city.

7 Pan on the Danforth
MAP F3 ▪ 516 Danforth Ave
▪ 416 466 8158 ▪ $

Familiar Greek favorites are served here, but lesser-known dishes such as *kakavia*, a fish stew, are standouts.

8 El Catrin
MAP E5 ▪ 18 Tank House Lane
▪ 416 203 2121 ▪ $$

Set in the old boiler house complex in the Distillery Historic District, this huge Mexican restaurant has wild Day of the Dead-themed decor.

Hand-painted wall mural, El Catrin

9 Hiro Sushi
MAP M4 ▪ 171 King St E
▪ 416 304 0550 ▪ $$

Diners feast on grilled tuna, *sashimi*, *wasabi*-spiked fish, and other Japanese delights, accompanied by fine sakes.

10 Gio Rana's Really, Really Nice Restaurant
MAP B4 ▪ 1220 Queen St E
▪ 416 469 5225 ▪ $$

This unconventionally named and decorated restaurant is housed in a former bank and specializes in great-value southern Italian fare.

See map on pp86–7

TOP10 Greater Toronto

The area surrounding the city proper has expanded rapidly in the last few decades, with suburban bedroom communities popping up around the urban fringe and engulfing fertile farmland. Although highway development ensures access to the many sites outside the city, roads can be extremely crowded at rush hour. Many parks and natural areas lie just outside the city, along with spacious beaches.

Artifact from Colborne Lodge

Toronto Zoo, set in the wilderness area of Rouge National Urban Park on the eastern edge of the city, is a delightful place to spend a day, as is, for family thrills, Canada's Wonderland. Historic attractions, such as Black Creek Pioneer Village, where costumed guides demonstrate pioneer life, offer a glimpse into 19th-century country life. Art lovers are drawn to the McMichael Canadian Art Collection in charming Kleinburg.

GREATER TORONTO

1 The Beach
MAP B2

Taking full advantage of its lakeside setting, The Beach feels more like a small resort town. In summer, crowds throng to the white-sand beaches, stroll the boardwalk, picnic in Kew Gardens, and go shopping along Queen Street. The area is at its busiest in late July, during the Beaches International Jazz Festival (see p63).

2 Ontario Science Centre
MAP B1 ▪ 770 Don Mills Rd ▪ 416 696 1000 ▪ Open 10am–4pm Mon–Fri (to 8pm Sat & 5pm Sun)

Exhibits here are interactive and geared toward youngsters. Eleven themed areas cover a diverse range of topics, including Earth's eco-systems, space, sport, communication, energy, and the human body.

Roller coaster, Canada's Wonderland

3 Canada's Wonderland
MAP A1 ▪ 9580 Jane St, Vaughan ▪ 905 832 8131 ▪ Open mid-Jun–Aug: 10am–10pm daily; Sep: 10am–8pm Sat & Sun; Oct: 10am–5pm Sat & Sun (hours subject to change) ▪ Adm ▪ www.canadaswonderland.com

This theme park north of Toronto draws crowds with over 200 attractions, 69 rides, and a water park. Thrills abound, the biggest pleasers being the roller coasters.

4 Toronto Zoo
MAP B1 ▪ 361A Old Finch Ave ▪ 416 392 5929 ▪ Open mid-Mar–Apr: 9:30am–4:30pm Mon–Fri, 9:30am–6pm Sat & Sun; May–Aug: 9am–7pm daily; Sep–Oct: 9:30am–4:30pm Mon–Fri, 9:30am–6pm Sat & Sun; Nov–mid-Mar: 9:30am–4:40pm daily ▪ Adm

This 710-acre (287-ha) zoo houses some 5,000 animals representing over 500 species. Large animals such as African elephants can be seen roaming in outdoor enclosures. Four tropical pavilions each represent a distinct geographic habitat.

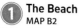

1	**Top 10 Sights** see pp95–7
①	**Restaurants** see p99
①	**Green Spaces** see p98

Pandas, Toronto Zoo

5 Black Creek Pioneer Village

MAP A1 ■ 1000 Murray Ross Pkwy ■ 416 736 1733 ■ Open May–Jun: 9:30am–4pm Mon–Fri, 11am–5pm Sat & Sun; Jul–Labour Day: 10am–5pm Mon–Fri, 11am–5pm Sat & Sun; Labour Day–Dec 25: 9:30am–4pm Mon–Fri, 11am–4:30pm Sat–Sun ■ Adm

For an authentic taste of early settler life in Canada, visit this re-creation of a 19th-century rural Ontario community. Among the dozens of buildings are a school, a church, village shops, houses, and barns. The grounds include an orchard, millpond, restored gardens, and grazing livestock. Costumed staff demonstrate pioneer crafts and carry out tasks such as tinsmithing and milling flour.

6 Aga Khan Museum

MAP B2 ■ 77 Wynford Dr ■ Open 10am–6pm Tue–Sun (until 8pm Thu) ■ Adm ■ www.agakhanmuseum.org

Housed in a distinctive angular building by Japanese architect Fumihiko Maki, the museum holds Islamic treasures, including ceramics, textiles, scientific texts, and musical instruments, as well as undiscovered masterpieces such as delicately painted folios from *Shahnameh* or Book of Kings (Iran, 16th century). The collection highlights the cultural diversity of Muslim society, from Spain, through Africa and the Middle East, to China.

R. C. HARRIS FILTRATION PLANT

Built in the late 1930s, this filtration plant has been dubbed the "palace of purification." Perched atop a gentle hill, this Art Deco structure holds the machines that treat the city's drinking water, which is pumped into the facility from a pipe that begins about 1.5 miles (2 km) offshore, in Lake Ontario. Nearly 200 million gallons (757 million litres) of water are processed daily, supplying about half of Toronto's needs.

7 McMichael Canadian Art Collection

MAP A1 ■ 10365 Islington Ave, Kleinburg, 18 miles (30 km) N of Toronto ■ 905 893 1121 ■ Open May–Oct: 10am–5pm daily; Nov–Apr: 10am–4pm ■ Adm

This outstanding gallery features a stellar display of works by the seminal Group of Seven painters, their contemporaries such as Tom Thomson and Emily Carr, and the artists they inspired. There's also an impressive collection of works by First Nations and Inuit artists.

McMichael Canadian Art Collection

8 Colborne Lodge

MAP A2 ■ Colborne Lodge Dr ■ 416 392 6916 ■ Open Jan, Feb & Apr: noon–4pm Sat & Sun; Mar: noon–4pm Thu–Sun; May–Aug: noon–5pm Tue–Sun; Sep: noon–5pm Sat & Sun; Oct–Dec: noon–4pm Tue–Sun ■ Adm

This 1837 house was the residence of land surveyor John Howard and his wife, Jemima. Howard deeded

The noteworthy exterior of the Aga Khan Museum

his estate to the city, thereby forming the basis for High Park (see p98). Located at the south end of the park, the Regency-style house, with its gorgeous circular verandah, has been fully restored and holds many of the Howards' original belongings, including John Howard's original watercolors of early Toronto scenes. Costumed guides lead tours. Don't miss the garden, planted with kitchen herbs and flowers.

Kids at the Legoland Discovery Centre

9 Legoland Discovery Centre

MAP A1 ▪ 1 Bass Pro Mills Dr, Vaughan ▪ 1 855 356 2150 ▪ Open 10am–7:30pm Mon–Thu, 10am–8pm Fri & Sat, 11am–7pm Sun (last admission 2 hours before closing) ▪ Adm

Little builders aged 3 to 10 will love this indoor complex packed with all things LEGO, including a Miniland of landmarks and a LEGO car speed test track. Adults unaccompanied by children will not be admitted.

10 Gibson House Museum

MAP A1 ▪ 5172 Yonge St ▪ 416 395 7432 ▪ Open 1–5pm Wed–Sun, 1–8pm Thu (Jul & Aug from 11am) ▪ Guided tours available ▪ Adm

This elegant Georgian farmhouse was built in 1851. The original owner, David Gibson, was a leader of the Upper Canada Rebellion in 1837 – he was forced to flee to the US when the uprising failed. Following his pardon, Gibson returned and built this home for his family.

A DAY AT THE BEACH

▶ MORNING

Start off your day with a great breakfast at the **Sunset Grill** (see p49) – the waffles are a local favorite. Cross the street and meander toward the lake through **Kew Gardens** (see p95), noting the unusual circular path and the rounded windows of the 1902 Kew Williams Cottage at the park's south end. Reaching the boardwalk, turn right and follow it to the end, a 15-minute stroll. Look out for the paved path on the right; take it into **Ashbridges Bay Park** (see p45), where you can stroll along the waterfront, watching sailboats moor and enjoying excellent views across the city from the west side. For lunch, retrace your steps to Kew Gardens, then up to Queen Street, for a famously good burger at Hero Certified Burgers (No. 2018). Eat in or take out and sit in Kew Gardens across the street.

AFTERNOON

Spend your afternoon browsing the shops on Queen Street E, maybe picking up a treat at The Nutty Chocolatier (No. 2179) to enjoy while taking a break at the serene sunken rock garden – Ivan Forrest Gardens – at Queen Street E and Glen Manor Drive. When shopped out, snag a seat on Outrigger's patio (No. 2232) and relax with a drink. If you're up for more walking, continue for another 10 minutes east to the **R. C. Harris Filtration Plant** (see p96) to stroll the grounds of this Art Deco gem and admire the view of the **Scarborough Bluffs** (see p98) and Lake Ontario.

See map on pp94–5 ←

Green Spaces

Birdlife, Rouge Urban Park

 Rouge National Urban Park
MAP B1 ■ www.rouge park.com

Following the course of the Rouge River, this is one of North America's largest urban parks. It contains the wildest natural area in the city *(see p45)*.

 Toronto Botanical Garden
MAP B1 ■ 777 Lawrence Ave E ■ 416 397 1340

Magnificent floral displays feature in this park by the Wilket Creek ravine.

③ **Humber Arboretum**
MAP A2 ■ 205 Humber College Blvd

Set near the West Humber River, this nature center has self-guided trails through woodlands and meadows, and exhibits on plants and wildlife.

④ **Martin Goodman Trail**
MAP A2–B2

Hugging the shore of Lake Ontario, the 35-mile (56-km) multiuse trail connects the waterfront parks.

⑤ **High Park**
MAP A2 ■ 1873 Bloor St W

Toronto's largest downtown park has long trails, along with play areas, tennis courts, a small zoo, and a snack bar and restaurant *(see p44)*.

High Park, a lovely green space

⑥ **Bluffer's Park**
MAP B2 ■ Brimley Rd, south end

Dramatic sandstone cliffs rise 350 ft (107 m) above Lake Ontario, providing a spectacular backdrop to this east-end park with a marina.

 Guildwood Park
MAP B1 ■ 201 Guildwood Pkwy

Enjoy gardens and naturalized areas full of woodland wild flowers at this Scarborough Bluff park. Intriguing architectural artifacts saved from demolished buildings are spread throughout the grounds.

⑧ **Humber Bay Butterfly Habitat**
MAP A2 ■ Humber Bay Park Rd E

Flowers and plants attract butterflies at this lakeshore park with a great view of the city's skyline. A demonstration garden highlights butterfly-attracting flowers for home gardens.

⑨ **Sunnybrook Park**
MAP B1 ■ Enter west of Leslie St via Wilket Creek Park

Encompassing shady Burke Ravine, this park provides respite from summer heat. There are interpretive nature trails, riding stables, sports fields, picnic tables, and a café.

 Kortright Center
MAP A1 ■ 9550 Pine Valley Dr, Woodbridge ■ 905 832 2289 ■ Adm

This conservation area has hands-on activities and guided nature walks – nighttime "owl prowls" are popular. Miles of trails lead through forests, meadows, and river valleylands.

Restaurants

① Chiu Chow Boy
MAP B1 ■ 3261 Kennedy Rd
■ 416 335 0336 ■ $

Chiu Chow Boy, in the far reaches of Scarborough, specializes in the cuisine of Chaozhou and is famous for its oyster omelets, marinated duck, and hand-shredded chicken.

② Scaramouche
MAP C2 ■ 1 Benvenuto Pl
■ 416 961 8011 ■ $$$ main room; $$ Pasta Bar

The Pasta Bar here is a city institution, and it is less pricey than the elegant main room, which has been serving up inventive cuisine for decades. Fabulous view of the city.

③ Chiado
MAP A3 ■ 864 College Street
■ 416 538 1910 ■ $$$

Excellent fresh seafood and hearty Portuguese meat dishes are served in an old-world, upscale dining room. Extensive Portuguese wine list.

④ North 44°
MAP B1 ■ 2537 Yonge St
■ 416 487 4897 ■ $$$

Chef Mark McEwan serves modern international cooking – French classics with sophisticated twists. An impressive drinks and wine list.

⑤ Katsura
MAP B1 ■ Westin Prince Hotel, 900 York Mills Rd ■ 416 444 2511 ■ $$

Japanese specialties such as sushi, *sashimi*, *tempura*, and grilled fish are served at the sushi bar, around *teppan* tables in the dining room, or in private *tatami* rooms.

⑥ Sushi Kaji
MAP A2 ■ 860 The Queensway
■ 416 252 2166 ■ $$$

Set-menu options, including the deluxe, chef's choice *omakase* menu, present course after course of wonderful, complex Japanese creations balanced with simple, incredibly fresh *sashimi* and sushi.

PRICE CATEGORIES
Price categories include a three-course meal for one, half a bottle of wine, and all unavoidable extra charges including tax.

$ under $50 $$ $50–$120 $$$ over $120

---

⑦ STACK
MAP B1 ■ 3265 Yonge St
■ 647 346 1416 ■ $$

Large restaurant offering southern barbecue, burgers, and doughnuts. The secret to its popularity is the perfect execution of a simple concept.

⑧ Auberge du Pommier
MAP B1 ■ 4150 Yonge St
■ 416 222 2220 ■ $$$

Classic French cooking with a contemporary twist. There are two intimate rooms, a bar, and a small patio. In winter, ask to sit by the fireplace.

Artistic dish, Auberge du Pommier

⑨ Via Allegro
MAP A2 ■ 1750 The Queensway ■ 416 622 6677 ■ $$

Authentic Italian food – pasta, seafood, and wood-fired oven pizzas – and an award-winning wine cellar, which, with over 5,000 selections, is an oenophile magnet.

⑩ Indian Street Food
MAP B2 ■ 1701 Bayview Ave
■ 416 322 3270 ■ $$

This bright and lively East York spot offers a modern slant on the meals found at Indian train stations. Try dishes such as charcoal-grilled prawns or chicken tikka. The no-tipping policy is a bonus.

See map on pp94–5

⭐🔟 Beyond Toronto

Within easy driving distance of Toronto are many delightful communities. North of the city, Honey Harbour and Gravenhurst are the gateways to cottage country, with beautiful lakes and forests, while Collingwood offers skiing in winter and summer fun on Georgian Bay. To the west of Toronto are many charming small towns, such as Stratford, with its world-renowned Shakespearean theater festival, and the Mennonite community of St. Jacobs. Further west, along the shores of Lake Huron, sandy beaches stretching north and south of the lovely town of Goderich beckon. The Niagara Peninsula, south and east, can easily fill a weekend, with attractions such as Niagara Falls and Ontario's best wine country.

Bust of Shakespeare

BEYOND TORONTO

1 Top 10 Sights
see pp101–103

① Restaurants
see p107

① Wineries
see p106

① Shops
see p105

① Country Stays
see p104

A horse-drawn carriage, a charming way to tour Niagara-on-the-Lake

1 Niagara-on-the-Lake

MAP Q3 ▪ Niagara Historical Museum: 43 Castlereagh St ▪ 905 468 3912 ▪ Open May–Oct: 10am–5pm daily; Nov–Apr: 1–5pm daily ▪ Adm

This charming historic town looks much as it did when built in the early to mid-1800s. Beautiful Georgian and Neo-Classical homes and quaint shops reward leisurely exploration. History buffs won't want to miss the Niagara Historical Museum, with exhibits on the region's fascinating past. The town is a good base for excursions along the scenic Niagara Parkway and to wineries *(see p106)*. It is also home to the summer Shaw Festival.

2 Niagara Falls

While the town itself sends kitsch to new heights, the falls are spectacular – truly a natural wonder and well worth the trip *(see pp34–5)*.

3 Stratford

MAP P2

Known globally for its Shakespeare festival, the city continues the theme of the bard with, among other things, a garden planted with some species named in his plays. Riverside parks are picnic-perfect; shops sell works by local artisans. Check out local history at Stratford-Perth Museum, and the fine High Victorian Perth County Court House (1887).

4 Gravenhurst

MAP Q1 ▪ Muskoka Steamships: www.realmuskoka.com ▪ Bethune Memorial House: 235 John St N, Gravenhurst, 705 687 4261, www.pc.gc.ca/bethune

Gravenhurst is a good base from which to explore the Muskoka region. It is also the departure point for lake cruises aboard an 1887 steamship. Stretching from Algonquin Park to Georgian Bay, Muskoka has over 1,600 lakes and rivers, and beaches that offer swimming opportunities.

Gravenhurst, a pretty lakeside town

5 Royal Botanical Gardens

MAP P3 ▪ 680 Plains Rd W, Burlington ▪ Open 10am–dusk daily

Four gardens and acres of nature sanctuaries are replete with greenhouses and trails. The world's largest lilac collection blooms in spring, and centuries-old roses thrive summer to fall. In winter, visitors enjoy the indoor Mediterranean Garden.

Maple Syrup Museum, St. Jacobs

6 St. Jacobs and Elora
MAP P2

Arts and crafts, antiques, and gift shops set in 19th-century buildings; bakeries; and cozy restaurants abound in these historic villages. Craft and food vendors at St. Jacobs' Farmers' Market (open year-round) include those offering the area's specialty, maple syrup, sold by local Mennonites. For more on this sweet treat, visit the Maple Syrup Museum at 1441 King Street N, St. Jacobs. A 15-mile (24-km) drive northeast is Elora, on the bank of the Grand River, and stunning Elora Gorge.

7 Georgian Bay Islands National Park
MAP P1 ▪ DayTripper: 705 526 8907 (reserve ahead)

Georgian Bay's rugged landscape is characterized by the windswept rock and pines of the Canadian Shield. Thousands of islands are scattered across the Bay, and some 59 make up the park. Access to the largest, Beausoleil, with its hiking trails, sandy beaches, forest, and a variety of reptiles and amphibians, is via a 15-minute boat ride aboard the *DayTripper* from the town of Honey Harbour.

8 Goderich
MAP N2 ▪ Huron County Museum: 110 North St, Open Jan–Apr: 10am–4:30pm Tue–Fri (until 8pm Thu), 1–4:30pm Sat; May–Dec: 10am–4:30pm Tue–Sat (until 8pm Thu), 1–4:30pm Sun ▪ Huron Historic Gaol: 181 Victoria St N, Open May–Aug: 10am–4:30pm Mon–Sat, 1–4:30pm Sun; Sep & Oct: 1–4pm Sun–Fri, 10am–4:30pm Sat, Adm ▪ Marine Museum: Open Jul & Aug: 1–4:30pm daily

Founded in 1827, this town on the shores of Lake Huron has a rich marine history and fine Victorian architecture. Its downtown streets radiate from an octagonal "square;" at its center is the Huron County Courthouse and Courthouse Park. The Huron County Museum has a fine collection of old farm equipment and military artifacts. Also of interest is the Huron Historic Gaol (built 1839–42) and the Marine Museum.

One of the tiny islands dotting Georgian Bay Islands National Park

⑨ Long Point Provincial Park

MAP P3 ▪ Hwy 59, 6 miles (10 km) **south of Port Rowan** ▪ 519 586 2133

This world-renowned refuge for migrating birds has been recognized by the United Nations as a biosphere reserve. Formed over thousands of years by sand washed from Lake Erie's shoreline, the 25-mile (40-km) sand spit has sand beaches and shallow waters. Spring and fall are idea for bird-watching; trails through dunes, forests, and wetlands can be enjoyed year-round. Camp sites have showers and electrical hook-ups.

A street in the heart of Collingwood

⑩ Collingwood

MAP P1 ▪ Blue Mountain Ski **Resort:** 705 445 0231 ▪ Scenic Caves **Nature Adventures:** 705 446 0256

This town takes full advantage of Niagara Escarpment scenery. A high point of the escarpment before it dips to Georgian Bay at Collingwood, nearby Blue Mountain is Ontario's best ski hill. At Scenic Caves Nature Adventures, walk Ontario's longest suspension footbridge or explore the limestone and ice caves.

A DRIVE IN THE COUNTRY

▶ MORNING

Start at **St. Jacobs Farmers' and Flea Markets**, admiring the handicrafts, collectibles, and foodstuffs of over 600 vendors. After stocking up on snacks, walk across the parking lot to the **Trolley Shop** for a 75-minute horse-drawn trolley tour through Mennonite country (Apr–Oct).

After the tour, drive to the Visitor Centre at 1406 King Street N; it features a short video on Mennonite history, photo exhibits, and a replica of a Mennonite Meetinghouse. When ready for lunch, head to Stone Crock *(No. 1396)*, for a country-style buffet.

AFTERNOON

Drive east on County Road 17; in a few miles you'll come to Road 22. Turn north to Route 86, then east on 86, watching for the sign to West Montrose. In this small town, look for the last remaining covered bridge in Ontario – called the kissing bridge by locals. The bridge crosses Grand River, a Heritage Waterway. Take Route 23 (turning into R21) north to charming **Elora**, 10 minutes away.

Browse its craft and antiques shops and admire the old limestone buildings before walking to the Elora Gorge Conservation Area to swim, hike, and enjoy your picnic snacks by the water.

Dinner is just a short drive away. Head down Route 18 to Fergus, rich both in Scottish history and late 19th-century architecture, to dine at the 1860s Breadalbane Inn *(487 St. Andrew Street W)*.

See map on p100 ←

Country Stays

1 Langdon Hall Country House Hotel & Spa
MAP P2 ▪ 1 Langdon Dr, RR 3, Cambridge ▪ 1 800 268 1898 ▪ www.langdonhall.ca ▪ $$

This hotel has well-appointed rooms, lovingly tended gardens, a spa, and fine cuisine (see p107).

2 Prince of Wales Hotel
MAP Q3 ▪ 6 Picton St, Niagara-on-the-Lake ▪ 1 888 669 5566 ▪ www.vintage-hotels.com ▪ $$

Impeccable service, opulent rooms, a spa, and a wine list to match the fabulous cuisine at this historic hotel in the heart of town.

A bedroom at the Prince of Wales

3 The Little Inn at Bayfield
MAP N2 ▪ 26 Main St, Bayfield ▪ 1 800 565 1832 ▪ www.littleinn.com ▪ $$

This historic inn near Lake Huron, first opened in 1832 as a coach house, justifiably prides itself on its fine restaurant and spa. Country antiques decorate the rooms.

4 Hockley Valley Resort
MAP P2 ▪ RR 1, Orangeville ▪ 519 942 0754 ▪ www.hockley.com ▪ $$

Nestled in a valley, this resort is a perfect base for pursuing outdoor activities such as downhill or cross-country skiing, golfing, tennis, and hiking. There is also a good spa.

5 Sherwood Inn
MAP Q1 ▪ 1090 Sherwood Rd, Port Carling ▪ 866 844 2228 ▪ www.sherwoodinn.ca ▪ $$

On the shores of Lake Joseph, this hotel with cottages makes an ideal base for outdoor pursuits.

6 Inn on the Twenty
MAP Q3 ▪ 3845 Main St, Jordan ▪ 1 800 701 8074 ▪ www.innonthetwenty.com ▪ $$

A luxurious inn with suites in the heart of Niagara wine country. Spa and winery packages are available.

7 Deerhurst Resort
MAP Q1 ▪ 1235 Deerhurst Dr, Huntsville ▪ 1 800 461 4393 ▪ www.deerhurstresort.com ▪ $$

This lakeside resort and spa, set on 800 acres (325 ha) of Muskoka countryside, is suitable for families and couples.

8 The Oban Inn
MAP Q3 ▪ 160 Front St, Niagara-on-the-Lake ▪ 866 359 6226 ▪ www.obaninn.ca ▪ $$

Overlooking Lake Ontario and surrounded by lush gardens, this inn has beautiful rooms and a fine restaurant. Short walk to the town.

9 Benmiller Inn
MAP N2 ▪ 81175 Benmiller Rd ▪ 1 800 265 1711 ▪ www.benmillerinnandspa.com ▪ $$

Close to the beaches of Lake Huron, this inn combines country charm and elegance. There's a spa too.

10 The Westover Inn
MAP P2 ▪ 300 Thomas St, St. Mary's ▪ 519 284 2977 ▪ www.westoverinn.com ▪ $$

In a quiet village, this Victorian house was once a seminary. It has comfortable rooms and extensive grounds.

For key to hotel prices see p116

Shops

1 Farmers' Markets
www.farmersmarketsontario.com

June to October, usually on Saturday mornings, local farmers sell fresh produce – fiddleheads, white asparagus, wild blueberries and mushrooms, and much more – at over 148 markets throughout Ontario.

2 Ontario Wines
Try award-winning wines at vineyards across the Niagara Peninsula before stocking up the cellar (see p106).

3 Craft Beer
MAP P2 ■ Neustadt Springs: 456 Jacob St, Neustadt ■ 519 799 5790

Ontario's microbreweries have enjoyed great popularity in recent years. Many, such as Neustadt Springs, offer tastings and tours.

4 Quilts
MAP P2 ■ Mennonite Quilts: 1389 King St N, St. Jacobs ■ 519 664 1817

The best place to buy these durable and gorgeous covers is St. Jacobs, where local Mennonite women still practice the traditional craft of hand-quilting. Stop in at Mennonite Quilts.

5 Factory Outlets
MAP Q3 ■ Canada One: 7500 Lundy's Lane, Niagara Falls ■ 905 356 8989

Snap up bargains on brands such as Guess, Roots, and Nike at Niagara Falls' outlet stores.

6 Fruits and Preserves
MAP Q3 ■ Greaves Jams and Marmalades: 55 Queen St, Niagara-on-the-Lake ■ 1 800 515 9939

In summer and fall, roadside stands in the Niagara region sell luscious fruits. Local companies turn these into jams, which are available at select stores. Greaves preserves are especially popular.

Greaves jam

7 Maple Syrup
The sap of Ontario's sugar maples is made into delicious pancake syrup and candies, sold at farmers' markets and shops.

8 Arts and Crafts
The work of Ontario's arts and crafts community – pottery, hand-blown glass, and jewelry – can be found across the province at fairs, markets, boutiques, and galleries.

9 Antiques
Hunting for vintage Canadian furniture, toys, silver, and china in Ontario towns is great sport. For a large selection, head to Erin, Jordan, St. Jacobs, Neustadt, and Elora.

10 Handmade Furniture
MAP P2

In southern Ontario, especially around Kitchener-Waterloo, Mennonite men craft durable country-style furniture from local woods. Watch for signs on the smaller roads pointing the way.

Mennonite quilter at work

See map on p100 ←

Wineries

① Vineland Estates Winery
MAP Q3 ▪ 3620 Moyer Rd, Vineland ▪ 1 888 846 3526

One of the most attractive wineries in the region, this vineyard has an 1857 stone carriage house, an excellent restaurant, and guided tours and tastings.

② Peller Estates Winery
MAP Q3 ▪ 290 John St E, Niagara-on-the-Lake ▪ 1 888 673 5537

Three generations of winemakers are behind this vineyard. Tours include a peek at the barrel-aging cellar. There is also a restaurant (see p107) and shop.

③ Trius Winery at Hillebrand
MAP Q3 ▪ 1249 Niagara Stone Rd, Niagara-on-the-Lake ▪ 1 800 582 8412

Along with estate tours and tastings, Trius hosts events, such as jazz and blues shows, in July and August.

④ Peninsula Ridge Estates Winery
MAP Q3 ▪ 5600 King St W, Beamsville ▪ 905 563 0900

The winemaker, local boy Jamie Evans, creates interesting blends; the whites are especially good. The restaurant (see p107) is set in a lovely Victorian house.

⑤ Inniskillin Wines
MAP Q3 ▪ Line 3, Service Rd 66, Niagara-on-the-Lake ▪ 1 888 466 4754

One of Ontario's oldest quality vineyards, established in 1975 and famous for its icewines, has guided tours. The shop and tasting bar are in a renovated 1920s barn.

⑥ Jackson-Triggs Vinters
MAP Q3 ▪ 2145 Niagara Stone Rd, Niagara-on-the-Lake ▪ 905 468 4637

This winery is one of the most technologically advanced facilities in the region. Tours and tastings.

⑦ Thirty Bench Wine Makers
MAP Q3 ▪ 4281 Mountainview Rd, Beamsville ▪ 905 563 1698

This little winery is known for its small lot, limited-production wines. Tastings are held in a rustic building overlooking the vineyards.

⑧ Malivoire Wine Company
MAP Q3 ▪ 4260 King St E, Beamsville ▪ 1 866 644 2244

In a region known primarily for its white wines, this organic vineyard produces excellent reds. A tasting room is set amid production tanks.

⑨ Reif Estate Winery
MAP Q3 ▪ 15608 Niagara Pkwy, Niagara-on-the-Lake ▪ 905 468 7738

This family winery has 125 acres (51 ha) of scenic vineyards. The boutique's design is inspired by an 1870s coach house. Daily tours are held in summer, and visitors can also enjoy the Wine Sensory Garden.

⑩ Château des Charmes
MAP Q3 ▪ 1025 York Rd, Niagara-on-the-Lake ▪ 905 262 4219

This family vineyard boasts over seven generations of wine-growing experience, with grapes harvested exclusively from their vineyards. There is a tasting bar, shop, and splendid rose garden.

Château des Charmes

Restaurants

1 **Eigensinn Farm**
MAP P1 ▪ RR 2, Singhampton
▪ 519 922 3128 ▪ $$$

Intimately gathered in chef Michael Stadländer's farmhouse, diners feast on exquisite, organic courses. Prices reflect the exclusive setting.

2 **Rundles**
MAP P2 ▪ 9 Cobourg St, Stratford ▪ 519 271 6442 ▪ Open May–Oct ▪ $$$

A Stratford institution serving classics such as grilled chicken and poached salmon, as well as a more adventurous gourmet menu.

Dining room, Peller Estates Winery

3 **Peller Estates Winery**
MAP Q3 ▪ 290 John St E, Niagara-on-the-Lake ▪ 1 888 673 5537 ▪ $$$

Enjoy the enchanting vineyard view (see p106) and the local, seasonal ingredients used in the five- and seven-course tasting menus.

4 **Langdon Hall**
MAP P2 ▪ 1 Langdon Dr, RR 3, Cambridge ▪ 1 800 268 1898 ▪ www. langdonhall.ca ▪ $$

Chef Jason Bangerter produces sublime dishes from iconic Canadian ingredients. The stately mansion might entice you to stay (see p104).

PRICE CATEGORIES

Price categories include a three-course meal for one, half a bottle of wine, and all unavoidable extra charges including tax.

$ under $50 **$$** $50–120 **$$$** over $120

5 **The Prune**
MAP P2 ▪ 151 Albert St (Shaw Club Hotel), Stratford ▪ 519 271 5052 ▪ Open late Apr–early Nov ▪ $$

Consistently excellent Canadian cuisine and outstanding wines. Diners decide the number of courses; the menu is fixed-price.

6 **Tiara**
MAP Q3 ▪ 155 Byron St, Niagara-on-the-Lake ▪ 905 468 2195 ▪ $$

In this upscale hotel restaurant savory roast and catch of the day join delights such as butter-poached lobster and rack-of-lamb on the menu.

7 **The Kitchen House at Peninsula Ridge**
MAP Q3 ▪ 5600 King St W, Beamsville ▪ 905 563 0900 ▪ $$

This restaurant offers fine dining in a gorgeous Queen Anne brick home atop a hill. Part of the Peninsula Ridge Estates Winery (see p106).

8 **Bijou**
MAP P2 ▪ 105 Erie St, Stratford ▪ 519 273 5000 ▪ $$

Quirky decor sets the stage for imaginative modern French dishes.

9 **Zees Grill**
MAP Q3 ▪ 92 Picton St, Niagara-on-the-Lake ▪ 905 468 5715 ▪ $$

The Niagara region is celebrated for its produce and wines, and Zees scores in both areas. There's a large patio, too.

10 **Thyme on 21**
MAP N2 ▪ 80 Hamilton St, Goderich ▪ 519 524 4171 ▪ $$

This unpretentious place is housed in a gorgeous Victorian home. The menu features traditional dishes.

See map on p100

Streetsmart

Flight Stop by Michael Snow, a 1979 sculpture depicting Canada geese in flight at the CF Toronto Eaton Centre

Getting To and Around Toronto

Arriving by Air

Pearson International Airport is the arrival point for most international visitors. Lying 16 miles (26 km) northwest of downtown, it is Canada's largest and busiest airport. Those flying shorter distances by turboprop may land at the much smaller **Billy Bishop Toronto City Airport**, located on the Toronto Islands near downtown.

The **UPExpress** train from Pearson takes 25 minutes to reach Union Station and runs every 15 minutes between 5:30am and 1am. Buy a **Presto** travel card for a discount. Use of the card is often confusing even for locals, and procedures are different depending on the transit system and vehicle, so check online for instructions.

At Pearson, limousines (flat rate) as well as taxis (both flat rate and metered) are plentiful outside the arrivals area (avoid drivers who tout inside the airport – they are usually unlicensed). Buses run by TTC, GO Transit, and others offer connections to alternative destinations in the region.

Billy Bishop Airport is connected by a ferry, free shuttle bus, and pedestrian tunnel. Both airports have car-rental booths.

Arriving by Rail

Union Station is Toronto's principal train station, and a hub for trains to the US and other parts of Canada, the subway, and regional **GO Transit** (Government of Ontario) buses. **Amtrak** and **VIA Rail** are great for train travel in the region.

Arriving by Bus

Greyhound and **Megabus** provide long-distance, economical bus services between Toronto and other cities. They arrive at and depart from the **Toronto Coach Terminal**.

Getting Around by Public Transit

The **Toronto Transit Corporation (TTC)** runs a well-integrated network of subways, buses, and streetcars. A single fare covers a trip of any distance within Toronto city and includes transfers (an extra fare is required beyond the city limits). Day and family passes offer savings, depending on the number of trips. Check the TTC website for rates and schedules.

Getting Around by Local Train

The GO Transit system is the regional service for the Greater Toronto and Hamilton area. It provides an excellent way to visit Niagara Falls, with direct trains on summer weekends, and a train-bus service at all other times.

Getting Around by Taxi

Cabs can be flagged down on most main downtown streets. Visitors can also order a cab over the telephone. Rates are set by the city. A tip for the driver is customary, usually 15–20 percent. Reliable cab companies include **Beck, Co-op, Crown**, and **Diamond. Uber** is a cheaper alternative.

Getting Around by Car

A driver's license valid in your own country is valid in Ontario for up to three months after you arrive. If you plan to stay longer, you will need to have an International Driver's Permit, which must be obtained in your home country before you arrive.

Insurance coverage for drivers is mandatory in Ontario; before leaving home, check your own policy to see if you are covered in a rental car. Most rental agencies will offer damage and liability insurance; it is a good idea to have both.

Toronto's roads are orderly but often very congested (Hwy 401 is the busiest road in North America), and parking in the city is expensive, making public transport a better choice. Most city attractions are accessible by transit, but a car may be convenient for outlying places such as the zoo, and will be useful for day trips to other destinations outside the city.

Using a mobile phone while behind the wheel is against the law. It is also illegal to pass a stopped streetcar until the doors have closed. The **Drive in Ontario** website offers useful information for visitors who plan to navigate the city by car.

Getting Around by Bicycle

Bike Share Toronto has sturdy rental bicycles stationed all over town. Pricing is economical if you make short trips between bike stations. If you keep the bike with you, extra fees quickly add up. Wearing a helmet is mandatory for children, but not for adults. Be wary of streetcar tracks, which can be a hazard.

Getting Around by Ferry

Ferries to the Toronto Islands depart from the foot of Bay Street. The trip is about 15 minutes. Get to the docks by taking the 509 Harbourfront or the 510 Spadina streetcar south to the Bay and Queens Quay stop, or the Bay bus No. 6 southbound from the corner of Front and Bay. Call or go online for **ferry schedules**.

Getting Around on Foot

Toronto is a walkable city. Streets are generally safe, and the grid layout makes navigation easy. In winter, escape the cold by going underground to the **PATH** system. Cross streets carefully at intersections or crosswalks, and be aware that drivers are permitted to turn right on a red light. They are supposed to yield right of way to pedestrians – but not all drivers do.

Bus and Boat Tours

CitySightseeing Toronto offers a combined boat and bus tour of downtown Toronto and the harbour. A combination deal adds Niagara Falls. Several companies, including **Get Your Guide**, **Toronto Harbour Cruises**, and **Toronto Tours** offer tours and cruises around the harbour and on Lake Ontario. It is also possible to book a day tour on board a three-masted schooner with **Tallship Cruises Toronto**.

DIRECTORY

ARRIVING BY AIR

Billy Bishop Toronto City Airport
w portstoronto.com/airport.aspx

Pearson International Airport
📞 416 247 7678, 1-866 207 1690 (for information about flights)
w torontopearson.com

Presto
w prestocard.ca

UPExpress
w upexpress.com

ARRIVING BY RAIL

Amtrak
w amtrak.ca

GO Transit
w gotransit.com

VIA Rail
w viarail.ca

ARRIVING BY BUS

Greyhound
w greyhound.ca

Megabus
w ca.megabus.com

Toronto Coach Terminal
610 Bay St
w torontocoachterminal.com

GETTING AROUND BY PUBLIC TRANSIT

Toronto Transit Corporation (TTC)
610 Bay St
w ttc.ca

GETTING AROUND BY TAXI

Beck
📞 416 751 5555

Co-op
📞 416 504 2667

Crown
📞 416 240 0000

Diamond
📞 416 366 6868

Uber
w uber.com/cities/toronto/

GETTING AROUND BY CAR

Drive in Ontario
w ontario.ca/page/drive-ontario-visitors

GETTING AROUND BY BICYCLE

Bike Share Toronto
w bikesharetoronto.com

GETTING AROUND BY FERRY

Ferry schedules
📞 416 392 8193
w www1.toronto.ca

GETTING AROUND ON FOOT

PATH
w torontopath.com

BUS AND BOAT TOURS

CitySightseeing Toronto
w citysightseeingtoronto.com

Get Your Guide
w getyourguide.com

Tallship Cruises Toronto
w tallshipcruisestoronto.com

Toronto Harbour Cruises
w torontoharbour.com

Toronto Tours
w torontotours.ca

Practical Information

Passports and Visas

A valid passport, with a visa when needed, must be presented by visitors upon entry to Canada. Residents of many countries, such as Australia, New Zealand, the US, and the majority of European countries, do not need a visa for Canada, but they do need an online Electronic Travel Authorization (eTA). Visitors may remain in Canada for up to six months. The **Visit Canada** website has useful information on visas.

In Toronto, the **British Consulate-General**, **US Consulate-General**, and **Australian Consulate-General**, among others, can provide consular services to their nationals.

Travel Safety Advice

Visitors can get up-to-date travel safety information from the **Australian Department of Foreign Affairs and Trade**, the **US Department of State**, and the **UK Foreign & Commonwealth Office**.

Customs and Immigration

Canada's rules governing what can be brought into the country are complex. In general, do not bring live animals, fresh fruit, vegetables, meat, dairy products, plants, or firearms into Canada without first obtaining authorization. Limited amounts of alcohol and tobacco may be imported duty-free by visitors who are of age (19 and 18 years old, respectively). Upon entry into Canada, if you are carrying any cash amount equal to or greater than $10,000, you must declare it.

Health

Unless your own health insurance covers medical costs while traveling, buying comprehensive health and dental insurance is strongly recommended: Canada does not provide medical services to visitors free of charge. Many credit card companies provide some degree of insurance; it is worthwhile checking this out before your trip.

Toronto does not pose many serious health hazards. However, the summer can be hot. Wear sunscreen. There are no venomous snakes in the Toronto area, and few dangerous insects, but mosquitoes are common and can be a nuisance in warm weather. Rabies outbreaks sometimes occur in Ontario. If you are bitten or scratched by an animal (domestic or wild), see a doctor immediately. The local wildlife usually stays away from humans, but keep your distance and don't touch any wild animals that seem "tame." If you visit forested or overgrown areas, watch out for giant hogweed and poison ivy, which can cause very painful blisters.

For minor ailments, pharmacists can be helpful. The majority of pharmacies are open from 9am to 9–10pm; some are open 24 hours a day. One of the most central is at **Shoppers Drug Mart** at Yonge and Carlton.

Hospitals in downtown Toronto include **Toronto General**, **St. Michael's**, **Mount Sinai**, the **Hospital for Sick Children**, and **Michael Garron Hospital**. Emergency treatment is available 24 hours a day.

For dental emergencies, the **Toronto Academy of Dentistry** emergency referral service links visitors with a nearby dentist after office hours. After midnight, go to an emergency room.

Emergency Services

If an emergency takes place, call the emergency service numbers. The city has a standard number for **ambulance**, **police**, and **fire**, as well as a **Toronto Police (non-emergency)** number and a tele-communications number for those who are **hearing impaired**.

Personal Security

Toronto is generally safe, but visitors should always stay alert. Thieves may operate in crowded places such as malls or big libraries. Pay attention to your surroundings and don't be distracted, especially if someone bumps into you. Don't carry more cash than you need and don't put your wallet in a back pocket. If you use a purse, ensure it closes tightly and remains in your sight. Be cautious at ATM machines. Watch your luggage carefully at airports and bus and train stations, and while checking in and out of hotels. Leave valuables in the hotel's safe.

Although the streets are generally safe, avoid dark places at night, especially if you are on your own. Carry a good map or GPS phone and check your route ahead of time. If you plan on returning late, make sure you have enough cash for a taxi.

Drinking

The legal drinking age in the province of Ontario is 19. Ontario has very strict laws about drinking in public: open bottles of alcohol are not allowed in public places. Fenced-off areas are set aside for selling and consuming alcohol at large events. Sales of wine, spirits, and beer are restricted to **LCBO** (Liquor Control Board of Ontario) outlets, and beer and coolers to **The Beer Store**. Domestic wines are also sold in small wine stores and some supermarkets.

Smoking

Toronto is a smoke-free city except in designated areas, and smoking is outlawed in vehicles carrying passengers under 16 years.

Disabled Accessibility

Bathrooms in some older buildings are often up or down stairs and not easily reached. Accessible streetcars are now starting to operate on the 510 Spadina and 509 Harbourfront routes. The subway is also becoming increasingly accessible, with more elevators to platforms and fully accessible ticket gates. All TTC buses are equipped with a ramp at the front door and have the ability to kneel.

Tourist Information

The **City of Toronto** and **Tourism Toronto** websites have useful information. Union Station has a visitor information booth, and also located here is the **Travellers' Aid Society**. **TripAdvisor Canada** offers good guides to Toronto, along with user reviews. Many shopping malls have booths with tourist information.

DIRECTORY

PASSPORTS AND VISAS

Australian Consulate-General
w canada.embassy.gov.au

British Consulate-General
w ukincanada.fco.gov.uk

US Consulate-General
w ca.usembassy.gov

Visit Canada
w cic.gc.ca/english/visit

TRAVEL SAFETY ADVICE

Australian Department of Foreign Affairs and Trade
w dfat.gov.au
w smartraveller.gov.au

UK Foreign & Commonwealth Office
w gov.uk/foreign-travel-advice

US Department of State
w travel.state.gov

HEALTH

Hospital for Sick Children
555 University Ave
c 416 813 1500
w sickkids.ca

Michael Garron Hospital
825 Coxwell Ave
c 416 461 8272
w tegh.on.ca

Mount Sinai
600 University Ave
c 416 586 5054
w mountsinai.on.ca

St. Michael's
30 Bond St
c 416 360 4000
w stmichaelshospital.com

Shoppers Drug Mart
465 Yonge St
c 416 408 4000
w shoppersdrugmart.ca

Toronto Academy of Dentistry
c 416 967 5649
w tordent.com

Toronto General
200 Elizabeth St
c 416 340 3946
w uhn.ca

EMERGENCY SERVICES

Ambulance, Fire, Police
c 911

Hearing Impaired
c 416 467 0493

Toronto Police (non-emergency)
c 416 808 2222
w torontopolice.on.ca

DRINKING

The Beer Store
w thebeerstore.ca

LCBO
w lcbo.com

TOURIST INFORMATION

City of Toronto
w toronto.ca

Tourism Toronto
w seetorontonow.com

Travellers' Aid Society
w travellersaid.ca

TripAdvisor Canada
w tripadvisor.ca

Currency and Banking

The unit of currency here is the Canadian dollar, which is divided into 100 cents. Coins are in denominations of 5, 10, and 25 cents, and 1 dollar (the loonie) and 2 dollars (the toonie). There is no 1 cent coin; change is rounded to the nearest 5 cents. Bank notes (bills) come in denominations of $5, $10, $20, $50, $100, and $500. Newer bills are plastic.

American coins will usually be accepted in shops, but will not work in any vending machines. Some shops will accept payment in US dollars as a courtesy, with an exchange rate shown at the till (change will be given in Canadian currency).

The best rate is generally available at one of Toronto's many banks or from the liquor or beer store. Rates at airport exchange booths are usually poor. Most bank, debit, and credit cards with security chips will work in Canada. Visa and MasterCard are more commonly accepted than American Express.

Canada's **Scotiabank** offers no-fee ATM withdrawals for customers of Westpac (Australia/NZ), Bank of America (US), Barclays (UK), and others.

Internet and Telephone

Free Wi-Fi is available in most hotels and many restaurants and coffee shops across the city. Wireless Toronto is a non-profit community group bringing Wi-Fi to as many public spaces in Toronto as possible.

Public telephones are becoming hard to find. Local calls cost 50 cents, and there is no limit on the duration of the call. For a long-distance number in North America, dial the prefix 1 and then the city code. To dial abroad, dial 011 + country code + city code.

Mobile phone services are expensive compared to the US and Europe, and are usually based around a long-term contract. However some providers, including **Fido** and **Koodo**, offer prepaid phone and Internet.

Check if your mobile phone provider offers service in Canada. For example, the UK's O2 and Orange networks works through Canada's **Rogers** network. If not, it may be possible to buy a prepaid SIM card before you come to Canada.

Postal Service

In Canada, post offices are normally located at a counter in pharmacies. However, you can often buy stamps at grocery stores and gas stations.

News and Media

Canada's main national newspaper is **The Globe and Mail**. The second-largest paper, with a more Toronto-centric slant, is the **Toronto Star**. Toronto weekly **Now** is available free at cafés, bars, bookstores, libraries, and street boxes throughout the city and is the best source for information on the local music and art scene. The monthly magazine **Toronto Life** is also helpful. Both are available online.

The national broadcaster **CBC** offers news on radio, TV, and its website. The popular **CBC Radio** gives a good feel for Canadian culture. For a sense of bustling Toronto, watch the news and magazine shows on **CityTV**.

Electrical Appliances

Canada's electrical supply conforms to the same standard used in the United States – 120 volts, 60 Hz. Many electronic devices will work with only a plug adapter. Other devices, such as hairdryers, may require a voltage converter. Converters are available at airports, train stations, and electronic stores, but research your requirements carefully before you leave home.

Time Difference

Toronto is in the Eastern Standard Time (EST) zone (5 hours behind London, England). Clocks switch to Daylight Saving Time (an hour forward) from the second Sunday in March to the first Sunday in November.

Weather

Its southern location and proximity to Lake Ontario make Toronto one of the warmer cities in Canada. Visitors are surprised by how hot and humid city summers can be. The sudden cooling in fall can produce spectacular changes in the colors of leaves (mid-October). In winter, temperatures often fall below freezing, and there can be snow and ice on the ground from December to March. Forecasts are usually in Celsius and in winter they will often include a "wind-chill" rating that factors in the extra cooling effect of wind on exposed skin.

Shopping

Most shops open 10am to 6pm, Monday to Saturday (often later on Thursday and Friday). Department stores and shops located in malls and commercial districts may keep longer hours, from 10am to 9pm Monday to Saturday, and between noon and 5pm Sunday. Widely observed retail holidays in Canada are January 1, July 1, Labour Day, Thanksgiving, and Christmas.

Look for end-of-season savings on merchandise. Excellent savings are to be had on Boxing Day (December 26), when prices on most goods are reduced dramatically.

In Canada, taxes are not included in the listed price unless specified, so when making a purchase always factor in an additional 13 percent HST (Harmonized Sales Tax). Items such as groceries are exempt from this tax, while others are taxed at a lower rate.

Accommodations

Toronto's big hotels are pricey, but you may find some bargains using **Kayak** and **Expedia**. Downtown has various budget hotels. Toronto also has many **Airbnb** offerings (often condos) at much lower prices.

Accommodations in Ontario are taxed with a 13 percent HST. An additional 3 percent destination tax is also levied on some hotel rooms in the City of Toronto. The website of the **Canada Revenue Agency** offers more details on this.

Hotel rates can vary according to the hotel category, the day of the week, and the season. Peak rates are weekdays and April to December. Rack rates (the basic room rates) are used in this book to provide a guide price. It is almost always possible to get a better deal, especially if you book online.

Porters and bellhops are tipped at least $1 per bag or suitcase, and chambermaids a minimum of $2–3 per day ($5 in high-end establishments). A hotel doorman will also appreciate a dollar or two for his services.

Dining

Most restaurants take reservations, and it is a good idea to book a table at popular dining spots well in advance. Mention if you have special needs or dietary requirements. It is considered good form to cancel your reservation if your plans change.

Service charges and tips are not usually added to dining bills. For service at restaurants, cafés, and clubs, plan on tipping about 15 percent of the pre-tax amount. At bars, leave a dollar or two for the bartender.

Breakfast is usually served in diners and coffee shops from about 6am to 10am. Lunch is available from about 11:30am to 2pm, and dinner between about 5pm and 10pm. Many restaurants and pubs offer a late-night menu. Brunches are often served on weekends only – and at some spots, on Sundays only – usually from 11am to 2pm or later. Some restaurants are closed on Sundays or Mondays, while others are closed on both days. Call ahead to check.

DIRECTORY

CURRENCY AND BANKING

Scotiabank
[w] scotiabank.com

INTERNET AND TELEPHONE

Fido
[w] fido.ca

Koodoo
[w] koodomobile.com

Rogers
[w] rogers.com

NEWS AND MEDIA

CBC and CBC Radio
[w] cbc.ca

CityTV
[w] citytv.com/toronto

The Globe and Mail
[w] theglobeandmail.com

Now
[w] nowtoronto.com

Toronto Life
[w] torontolife.com

Toronto Star
[w] thestar.com

ACCOMMODATIONS

Airbnb
[w] airbnb.ca/toronto

Canada Revenue Agency
[w] cra-arc.gc.ca

Expedia
[w] expedia.com

Kayak
[w] kayak.com

Places to Stay

PRICE CATEGORIES
For a standard double room per night (with breakfast
if included), taxes, and extra charges.

$ under $175 $$ $175–350 $$$ over $350

Luxury Hotels

The Omni King Edward Hotel
MAP L4 ■ 37 King St E
■ 416 863 9700 ■ www.
omnihotels.com/hotels/
toronto-king-edward ■ $$
Opened in 1903, this
grand hotel, affectionately
called "the King Eddy,"
offers elegantly appointed
rooms, courteous service,
a spa, and every possible
amenity guests may need.

Park Hyatt Toronto
MAP C3 ■ 4 Avenue Rd
■ 416 925 1234 ■ toronto.
park.hyatt.com ■ $$
Luxurious, spacious
rooms with marble bath-
rooms and free high-
speed Internet, attentive
service, and a central
Yorkville location make
this classy hotel a great
favorite. The Hyatt's Roof
Lounge (see p57) provides
guests with a spectacular
view of the city, and the
posh Stillwater Spa is
one of the city's best.

Delta Toronto Hotel
MAP K5 ■ 75 Lower
Simcoe St ■ 416 849 1200
■ www.marriott.com
■ $$$
Set right in the heart of
the Harbourfront district
and connected to Union
Station and the PATH
system, the hotel offers
spectacular lake views.
Amenities include a
24-hour gym with a CN
Tower view. Ultramodern
and super friendly.

Fairmont Royal York
MAP K5 ■ 100 Front St W
■ 416 368 2511 ■ www.
fairmont.com/royal-york-
toronto/ ■ $$$
Opposite Union Station,
this large hotel has been
a Toronto landmark since
1929. The magnificent
lobby is a fitting backdrop
for the heads of state who
have stayed here. There
are several restaurants
and bars, including the
cozy Library Bar (see p72),
and a great spa.

Ritz-Carlton Hotel
MAP J4 ■ 181 Wellington
St W ■ 416 585 2500
■ www.ritzcarlton.com/
en/hotels/canada/toronto
■ $$$
A five-star hotel, the Ritz-
Carlton is set in the heart
of the theater district and
overlooks the red carpet
during the popular
Toronto International Film
Festival. It is known for
pampering its guests,
including children ("Ritz
Kids"). The club-level
rooms are luxurious.

Shangri-la Hotel
MAP K4 ■ 188 University
Ave ■ 647 788 8888
■ www.shangri-la.com/
toronto ■ $$$
This luxurious hotel
spans 17 floors and
has a distinctly Asian
aesthetic – raw silk
wall coverings, a patio
with a Japanese garden,
and tea libraries. Rooms
are exceptionally smart
and modern.

Business-Friendly Hotels

DoubleTree by Hilton Hotel Toronto Downtown
MAP K3 ■ 108 Chestnut St
■ 416 977 5000 ■ double
tree3.hilton.com ■ $$
Contemporary decor and
luxurious touches pamper
travelers. Restaurants Lai
Wah Heen (see p54) and
Hemispheres add to the
pleasure of a stay here.

The Suites at One King West
MAP K4 ■ 1 King St W
■ 416 548 8100 ■ www.
onekingwest.com ■ $$
Located in the Financial
District, this hotel is
uniquely built atop a 1914
building that once housed
the Dominion Bank of
Canada. The hotel has a
24-hour business center,
bistro, and private club.
The views are amazing.

Toronto Marriott Downtown Eaton Centre
MAP K3 ■ 525 Bay St
■ 416 597 9200 ■ www.
marriott.com ■ $$
Featuring a full business
center with secretarial
service, dedicated
business guestrooms,
and 18 meeting rooms,
this 18-story hotel is
conveniently located next
to the CF Toronto Eaton
Centre (see pp30–31).

Westin Bristol Place Toronto Airport
MAP A2 ■ 950 Dixon Rd
■ 416 675 9444 ■ www.
westintorontoairport.
com ■ $$
Just five minutes from
Pearson Airport, the hotel

surprises at check-in with a waterfall in its lobby. Guests appreciate the modern, spacious rooms, personalized service, fitness center, indoor pool, and other amenities.

Westin Harbour Castle

MAP K6 ▪ 1 Harbour Sq ▪ 416 869 1600 ▪ www. westinharbourcastle toronto.com ▪ $$
With a location right on Lake Ontario, yet close to downtown, this high-rise hotel offers stunning views from its ample rooms. Facilities include a pool, fitness room, outdoor tennis court, spacious meeting rooms, and full business service.

Hilton Toronto

MAP K4 ▪ 145 Richmond St W ▪ 416 869 3456 ▪ www3.hilton.com ▪ $$$
In the financial district, this business hotel has spacious standard rooms, suites ideal for longer stays, and executive rooms with extras such as special work chairs.

InterContinental Toronto Centre

MAP J5 ▪ 225 Front St W ▪ 416 597 1400 ▪ www. torontocentre.inter continental.com ▪ $$$
Attached to Toronto's Convention Centre, this hotel provides attentive service and excellent business facilities. The eighth floor is for Priority Club business guests.

Sheraton Centre

MAP K4 ▪ 123 Queen St W ▪ 416 361 1000 ▪ www. sheratontoronto.com ▪ $$$
Steps from City Hall, this hotel complex bustles

with conventioneers and tour groups. There are 1,377 rooms and good, efficient service.

Boutique Hotels

Madison Manor

MAP C3 ▪ 20 Madison Ave ▪ 416 922 5579 ▪ www.madisonmanor boutiquehotel.com ▪ $
Featuring many unusual details, including alcove windows and fireplaces, this lovingly restored Victorian mansion aims to make its guests feel as though they have stepped into a picturesque English country inn.

Broadview Hotel

MAP F4 ▪ 106 Broadview Ave ▪ 416 362 8439 ▪ www.thebroadview hotel.ca ▪ $$
Set in a meticulously restored 125-year-old Romanesque Revival building, this 58-room hotel boasts a grand facade and hip interior design.There is a cafe, a restaurant, and a rooftop bar with stunning views.

Gladstone Hotel

MAP K4 ▪ 1214 Queen St W ▪ 416 531 4635 ▪ www.gladstonehotel. com ▪ $$
The artist-designed rooms at this trendy, welcoming hotel are compact but comfortable. The hotel hosts arts events, and has a lively bar and café.

The Old Mill Inn

MAP A2 ▪ 21 Old Mill Rd ▪ 416 236 2641 ▪ www.oldmilltoronto. com ▪ $$
This inn on the Humber River is a 15-minute drive west of downtown

(20 minutes by subway from Yonge and Bloor). All 44 rooms overlook the river; the 13 suites are located in the historic old mill building. All the rooms are spacious and luxurious, and there's a relaxing spa and rejuvenating wellness center, too.

The Hazelton

MAP C3 ▪ 118 Yorkville Ave ▪ 416 963 6300 ▪ www.thehazelton hotel.com ▪ $$$
A favorite with jetsetters, Toronto's first five-star hotel is located in the heart of upscale Yorkville. It boasts glamorous Hollywood-style rooms and the city's best celebrity-spotting bar.

SoHo Metropolitan

MAP J4 ▪ 318 Wellington St W ▪ 416 599 8800 ▪ www.metropolitan. com/soho ▪ $$$
Lovers of luxury will adore this boutique hotel in the Entertainment District. Duvets, walk-in closets, extravagant bathrooms with heated marble floors, and many high-tech gadgets are available as standard.

Windsor Arms

MAP C3 ▪ 18 Thomas St ▪ 416 971 9666 ▪ www. windsorarmshotel.com ▪ $$$
Personal service is writ large in this elegant hotel with just 28 guest rooms on the first four floors of a 14-story building. Guests enjoy the two-floor spa and delight in the cuisine of Courtyard Café. There is also a popular steakhouse and tearoom.

For a key to hotel price categories see p116

Bed and Breakfasts

Au Petit Paris
MAP D3 ▪ 3 Selby St
▪ 416 928 1348 ▪ www.
aupetitparis.ca ▪ $
Just east of downtown and
within a 15-minute walk of
the upscale shops on Bloor
Street and in Yorkville, this
B&B has a Parisian flair.
Its four rooms, all with
private baths, are deco-
rated in shades of ocher
and red. Breakfast can be
taken on the rooftop patio.

Making Waves Boatel
MAP H6 ▪ 539 Queens
Quay W ▪ 647 403 2764
▪ www.boatel.ca ▪ $
Be lulled to sleep in the lap
of Lake Ontario. Set right in
the Harbourfront marina,
this moored boat has two
cabins with a shared bath,
and a larger stateroom
with private bath. Enjoy
evening drinks under the
stars on the Sky Lounge.

McGill Inn
MAP L2 ▪ 110 McGill St
▪ 416 351 1503 ▪ $
Reasonable prices and
eight tastefully decorated
rooms, some with shared
baths, and make this B&B
in a restored Victorian
townhouse a good choice
for the budget-conscious
traveler. It is a 10-minute
walk away from the CF
Toronto Eaton Centre.

Pimblett's Downtown
Toronto B&B
MAP E4 ▪ 242 Gerrard
St E ▪ 416 921 6898
▪ www.pimblett.ca ▪ $
These five cozy rooms in a
Victorian house are deco-
rated to the nines with all
things British, ranging from
antiques to bric-a-brac,
offering an unforgettably
eccentric stay in Cabbagetown. Geoffrey Pimblett,

the owner, amuses guests
with impressions of the
Queen of England.

Smiley's B&B
MAP D6 ▪ 4 Dacotah Ave
▪ 416 203 8599 ▪ www.
eralda.ca ▪ $
Snuggle up in the rooftop
Belvedere Room of this
Algonquin Island cottage.
Have breakfast with your
hosts, appreciate the
tranquility, and explore
Toronto Islands. A studio
that sleeps four is
available in summers.

Annex Garden B&B
MAP B3 ▪ 445 Euclid Ave
▪ 416 258 1179 ▪ www.
annexgarden.com ▪ $$
Stay in a historic house in
Little Italy, an unbeatable
location. Two apartments
and two rooms are avail-
able in this spiffy home
that boasts four fireplaces
and underfloor heating.

By the Park Bed
& Breakfast
MAP A2 ▪ 92 Indian
Grove ▪ 416 520 6102
▪ www.bythepark.ca ▪ $$
In this restored 1910 home,
rooms are large and bath-
rooms are luxurious. You
can unwind in the beautiful
garden or warm up by one
of the fireplaces, depending
on the season. The price
includes a delicious
home-cooked vegan
or vegetarian breakfast.

Mid-Range Hotels

Eaton Chelsea
MAP L2 ▪ 33 Gerrard St W
▪ 416 595 1975 ▪ www.
eatonhotels.com ▪ $$
Canada's biggest hotel,
with 1,590 guest rooms,
the Eaton Chelsea caters
equally well to business
travelers and families. An
indoor waterslide, the Kid

Centre, and a teen lounge
with Xboxes, and a pool
table go a long way to
keeping all ages amused.

Hotel Victoria
MAP L4 ▪ 56 Yonge St
▪ 416 363 1666 ▪ www.
hotelvictoria-toronto.
com ▪ $$
Steps from Union Station
in the city's Financial
District, this 56-room
hotel offers the amenities
of a large hotel along with
excellent service. Close to
many top attractions.

International
Plaza Hotel
MAP A2 ▪ 655 Dixon Rd
▪ 416 244 1711 ▪ www.
internationalplazahotel.
com ▪ $$
Near Pearson Airport,
this hotel has 433 well-
appointed guestrooms.
A variety of restaurants
and cafés, along with a
spa, a fitness center, and
an indoor swimming pool
with waterslides, ensure
you rarely need leave the
premises. Also a popular
conference center.

Novotel Toronto
Centre
MAP L5 ▪ 45 The
Esplanade ▪ 416 367 8900
▪ www.novotel.com ▪ $$
Well placed near many
downtown attractions,
this Novotel is a good
example of the French
chain. The large rooms
are functional, and there
is a lovely lobby, fitness
room, and indoor pool.

Radisson Plaza Hotel
Admiral Toronto
Harbourfront
MAP J6 ▪ 294 Queens
Quay W ▪ 416 203 3333
▪ www.radisson.com ▪ $$
Bright, large rooms in this
hotel, steps from Lake

Ontario and harbourfront attractions, appeal to both business and leisure travelers alike. There is a good restaurant, and a rooftop pool and deck that overlooks the lake.

Hyatt Regency Toronto

MAP J4 ■ 370 King St W ■ 416 343 1234 ■ www. torontoregency.hyatt. com ■ $$$

The extensively renovated Hyatt Regency is situated close to the city's Entertainment District. The rooms look out over downtown Toronto and Lake Ontario.

Budget Hotels and Accommodations

Bond Place Hotel

MAP D4 ■ 65 Dundas St E ■ 416 362 6061 ■ www. bondplace.ca ■ $

Ideally located right in the heart of downtown Toronto, this hotel is close to the CF Toronto Eaton Centre, the theater district, and many other local attractions. The rooms are modern and well equipped, and the hotel has a restaurant.

Hostelling International Niagara Falls

MAP Q3 ■ 4549 Cataract Ave, Niagara Falls ■ 905 357 0770 ■ www.hostellingniagara. com ■ $

Located just a short walk away from the falls, this hostel is especially well kept. There are a few private rooms, along with dorms and some four-bed rooms (no private baths).

Hostelling International Toronto

MAP L4 ■ 76 Church St ■ 416 971 4440 ■ www. hostelling toronto.com ■ $

Located just south of the Gay Village, this hostel provides one of the city's cheapest stays, with mainly shared rooms in dorms. A few private rooms with en suite are also available.

Marriott Gateway on the Falls

MAP Q3 ■ 6755 Fallsview Blvd, Niagara Falls ■ 1 800 618 9059 ■ www.marriott.com ■ $

The east-facing rooms in this comfortable high-rise hotel offer glorious views of Niagara Falls. Hotel staff are extremely helpful and knowledgeable, and the rooms are large and well appointed.

Neill-Wycik College Hotel

MAP M2 ■ 96 Gerrard St E ■ 416 977 2320 ■ www.neill-wycik.com ■ $

This student residence turns into a guesthouse from early May to the end of August. While the rooms are spartan and the bathrooms are shared, the price is right for tight budgets. Groups are welcome. The central location means many of the city's top destinations are in walking distance. Breakfast is included.

The Planet Traveler Hostel

MAP H2 ■ 357 College St ■ 647 352 8747 ■ www.theplanettraveler. com ■ $

Housed in a 100-year-old building, this spacious,

clean and conveniently located accommodation is Canada's greenest hostel. It has a rooftop bar.

Victoria's Mansion Inn and Guest House

MAP L1 ■ 68 Gloucester St ■ 416 921 4625 ■ www. victoriasmansion.com ■ $

On a tree-lined street in the heart of Toronto's Gay and Lesbian Village, this charming small hotel, with a lovely Victorian-style garden, provides a respite from the bustle of the city. All rooms come with private baths, and suites are equipped with a fridge and microwave. Free parking.

Victoria University

MAP D3 ■ 140 Charles St W ■ 416 585 4524 ■ www.vicu.utoronto.ca ■ $

Located on the campus of the University of Toronto, Victoria University opens its doors to budget travelers during summer-semester holidays from mid-May to the end of August. A quiet setting combined with a central location make these lodgings an excellent base from which to explore the city.

Cambridge Suites

MAP L4 ■ 15 Richmond St E ■ 416 368 1990 ■ www. cambridgesuitestoronto. com ■ $$

Excellent service is standard at this hotel, which offers two-room suites only. The fully equipped work areas have all the bells and whistles. A microwave, fridge, and coffee machine in every suite ensure you have all you need for your stay.

For a key to hotel price categories see p116

Index

Acknowledgments

Author

Lorraine Johnson is the author of several books and co-author or DK's Eyewitness Guide to Chicago. She lives in Toronto.

Barbara Hopkinson is a Toronto-based writer and editor who has directed a wide range of international projects.

Additional contributor
Dan Liebman

Publishing Director Georgina Dee

Publisher Vivien Antwi

Design Director Phil Ormerod

Editorial Ankita Awasthi Tröger, Avanika, Rachel Fox, Maresa Manara, Sally Schafer, Jackie Staddon, Rachel Thompson

Design Tessa Bindloss, Vinita Venugopal.

Commissioned Photography Rough Guides / Enrique Uranga

Picture Research Susie Peachey, Ellen Root, Lucy Sienkowska

Cartography Dominic Beddow, Simonetta Giori, Mohammad Hassan, Casper Morris

DTP Jason Little

Production Poppy Werder-Harris

Factchecker Taraneh Jerven

Proofreader Clare Peel

Indexer Helen Peters

First edition created by International Book Productions Inc., Toronto

Picture Credits

The publisher would like to thank the following for their kind permission to reproduce their photographs:
Key: a-above; b-below/bottom; c-centre; f-far; l-left; r-right; t-top

123RF.com: Lin Chu-Wen 75cra; Adrian Wojcik 4clb; yelo34 66tl.

Adelaide Hall/Strut Entertainment: Matt Vardy 57tr.

Agha Khan Museum: Janet Kimber 61cl, 96b; Tom Arban Photography 41cl.

Alamy Stock Photo: All Canada Photos / Klaus Lang 1, 30–31, / Rolf Hicker 35tl; Jon Bilous 22–3; Bill Brooks 17tl, 19tl, 19clb; Lorne Chapman 3tl, 64–5; Cosmo Condina 4crb; Cosmo Condina North America 35cr; Elena Elisseeva 7tr; Gaertner 13bl, 105bl; Bert Hoferichter 18c; Nick Jene 57clb; maximimages.com 68cla; Henk Meijer 10cl; Jill Morgan 10crb; National Geographic Creative / Richard Nowitz 16cb; Nikreates 33bl; REUTERS / Roger Bacon 62br; robertharding / Stuart Dee 77bl; Andrew Rubtsov 4cla, 14cl; adiseshan shankar 15tr; Rosemarie Stennull 69cl, 102–3; Tolbert Photo 4b; Torontonian 3tr, 4t, 108–9; Arsalan Uljamil 35clb; Janusz Wrobel 43tr.

ALO Restaurant: 56bl.

Art Gallery Of Toronto: 4cr.

Aunties & Uncles: 54ca.

AWL Images: Alan Copson 34bl.

Bridgeman Images: Art Gallery of Ontario, Toronto, Canada / *Eve* (c.1883) by Auguste Rodin10bl, *Western Forest* (c.1931) by Emily Carr 20cl, / *Figure with Ulu* (1966) by Aqjangajuk Shaa, 20br, / *Autumn Leaves, Batchewana, Algoma* (c.1919) by James Edward Hervey Macdonald 20–21; *Venus Simultaneous* (1962) by Michael Snow 21tl; / *The Concert* (1918–19) by Pierre Auguste Renoir 21cr; / *Hina and Fatu* (c.1892) by Paul Gauguin 74tr.

Buca/Gab Communications: Rick O'Brien 83b.

Buddies in Bad Times Theatre: 53b.

Cafe é Diplomatico/Branding and Buzzing: 82tr.

Caffe Furbo: Kevin Bonnici 27bl.

Canada Opera Company: Sam Javanrouh 51cl.

Canada's Wonderland: 95tr; Graig Abel 48b.

The Ceili Cottage: 92cra.

CF Toronto Eaton Centre: 11cr.

Château des Charmes: 106b.

City Of Toronto Historic Sites: 78cra, 86tl, 94tl, 78cra; Summer Leigh Photography 68b.

Coal Miner's Daughter: 80br.

Corkin Gallery: artist on display David Urban 26cl.

Courtesy of the Thomas Fisher Rare Book Library, University of Toronto: 60tl.

courtesy of Design Exchange: 70t.

Drake Hotel Properties: 81cr.

Dreamstime.com: Alexsvirid 47b; Amarita 55br; Appalachianviews 31tl, 44cla, 44–5, 46bl, 58b, 87tl; Artemzavarzin 16–17; Bokdavid 37tl; Canadapanda 63clb; Catstail 47cr; Clivechilvers 63br; Daddiomanottawa 36cla; Deymos 59tl; Elenathewise 4cl, 103cl; Erandalx 43bl; Fabry10 17cl; Flusvarghi 98b; Harryfn 42bl; Helgidinson 58cla; Iwhitwo 101c; Javenlin1018 15b, 24cl; Koco77 30clb; Lagron49 48ca; Lester69 60b; Chu-wen Lin 7br; Mark52 2tl, 8–9; Maudem 42t; Mikecphoto 18br, 36bc; Noodles73 41tr; Pixart 11br; Rabbit75 34–5; Sampete 16cl, 31bl, 78bl; Vdvtut 61tr; Vitaldrum 11tl; Wickedgood 45tr; Yelo34 12–13, 13cra.

El Catrin/Distillery Restaurant Corporation: 93cr.

Gadabout: Charlotte Giacomelli 91clb.

Gardiner Museum: Melissa Shimmerman 40ca.

Getty Images: Education Images 102tl; William England 37bl; Rick Gerharter 52clb; LightRocket / Roberto Machado Noa 76cb, / Wolfgang Kaehler 100tl; Panoramic Images 76t; Brian Summers 87crb; Toronto Star / Todd Korol 89clb.

Greaves Jams: 105ca.

Harbourfront Centre: 67tl.

Hockey Hall of Fame: 32clb; AJ Messier Photography 32–3, 33cr; Matthew Manor 11clb.

iStockphoto.com: bakerjarvis 88t; Kenneth Cheung 19cla; JavenLin 2tr, 38–9; Orchidpoet 84–5, 101clb.

Julie's Cuban: Parisa Almasi 82clb.

Le Sélect Bistro: 54b.

Legoland Discovery Centre/Enterprise Canada: 97cla.

Liberty Group: 10br; Lorne Chapman 24br, 24–5, 25tl, 25crb.

Lula Lounge: 56t.

Marben: Rick O'Brien 73cla.

McMichael Canadian Art Collection: 96c.

Mercatto Restaurant Group: 73crb.

Mirvish.com: Edward Burtynsky 71cr; Paul Coltas 71bl.

Morba: 80ca.

National Ballet of Canada: *Elena Lobsanova and Guillaume Côté in Romeo and Juliet* photo Bruce Zinger 51tr.

NXNE Festival/Flip Publicity: 62t.

Old Spaghetti Factory: 49br.

images courtesy of Oliver & Bonacini Restaurants: Cindy La 99crb.

Omni King Edward Hotel: 92bl.

Ontario Heritage Trust: Peter Lusztyk 50t.

Ontario Science Centre: 40–41.

The Oxley Public House/Broadcloth Hospitality: 81tr.

Peller Estates Winery and Restaurant: Cosmo Condina 107clb.

Prince of Wales Hotel/Vintage Hotels: 104cl.

Pusateri's Fine Foods: 79cb.

Ripley's Aquarium of Canada: 6cla, 11cla, 28cl, 28crb, 29cr, Michael Hope 28–9, 29br.

Robert Harding Picture Library: Jean B. Heguy 67br.

Roots: 79tr.

Rouge National Urban Park: Parks Canada 98tl, / M Ruston 45cl.

Royal Ontario Museum: 10cra, 12clb; Brian Boyle 14tc.

St. Lawrence Market Complex: City Of Toronto / Jose San Juan 90t.

The Chase: Brandon Barre 55tl, 72b.

The Royal Conservatory: Tom Arban 50bl.

Toronto Zoo: 49tl, 95br.

Tourism Toronto: Marketing Department of the The Distillery Historic District 26–7.

Young Centre for the Performing Arts: Tom Arban 27tl.

Cover

Front and spine: **Alamy Stock Photo:** Henk Meijer.
Back: **Dreamstime.com:** Ron Sumners.

Pull Out Map Cover

Alamy Stock Photo: Henk Meijer

All other images © Dorling Kindersley
For further information see:
www.dkimages.com

As a guide to abbreviations in visitor information blocks: **Adm** = admission charge; **DA** = disabled access; **D** = dinner; **L** = lunch.

Penguin Random House

Printed and bound in China

First American edition, 2012
Published in the United States by
DK Publishing, 345 Hudson Street,
New York, New York 10014

Copyright 2005, 2018 © Dorling
Kindersley Limited

A Penguin Random House Company

18 19 20 21 10 9 8 7 6 5 4 3 2 1

**Reprinted with revisions 2007,
2009, 2011, 2013, 2015, 2018**

Published in Great Britain by Dorling
Kindersley Limited.

A catalog record for this book is available
from the Library of Congress.

ISSN 1479-344X

ISBN 978 1 4654 6765 2

FSC MIX
Paper from
responsible sources
www.fsc.org FSC™ C018179

SPECIAL EDITIONS OF DK TRAVEL GUIDES

DK Travel Guides can be purchased
in bulk quantities at discounted prices
for use in promotions or as premiums.
We are also able to offer special
editions and personalized jackets,
corporate imprints, and excerpts from
all of our books, tailored specifically to
meet your own needs.

To find out more, please contact:

in the US
specialsales@dk.com

in the UK
travelguides@uk.dk.com

in Canada
specialmarkets@dk.com

in Australia
**penguincorporatesales@
penguinrandomhouse.com.au**

Toronto Sight Index

Toronto Selected Sight Index